SILVER BULLETS

A GUIDE TO INITIATIVE PROBLEMS, ADVENTURE GAMES, STUNTS AND TRUST ACTIVITIES by Karl Rohnke

Written by Karl Rohnke. Published by Project Adventure, Inc.

All photographs by the author except where noted.

Printed by Wilkscraft Creative Printing, Beverly, Massachusetts.
Manufactured in the United States of America
Copyright © 1984 by Project Adventure, Inc.
Sixth Printing April 1988

To those hundreds of Project Adventure workshop participants who said (or thought) "NO WAY"— and then found a way.

Table of Contents

Games **14**

Toss-a-Name Game 17
Frantic 18
Balloon Frantic 19
Smokestack 20
Paul's Balls 21
Tattoo 22
Mine Field 24
Physics Phantasy 25
Comet Ball Horseshoes 25
Ultimate Comet Ball 25
Mirrors & Mortars 26
Fast Draw 28
Off the Wall 29
Frisbee Shuffleboard 30
Sardines 30
Moonball 31
Paper Golf 32
Which Way? Softball 34
Impulse 35
Body English 35
Unholy Alliance 36
Shoot Out 39
Sit Down Dodge Ball 40
Full House 40
Boffer Bonkers 41
Tusker 42
Samurai & Kamikaze Variation 45
Texas Big Foot 46
Tickle-a-Pickle 46
Shark 47
Tug-o-War 47
Cat & Mouse 47
Where-am-I? 47
Booop 49
Braaaaaaack-Whfffff 50
Fire In The Hole 51
Basic Killer 52
Hands Down 53
Bang, You're Dead 54
Passing Crossed Or Uncrossed 55
I've Got the Beat 55
Nerf Ball Knockaround 56
Tegwar 56
Trash Ball 57
Rodeo Throw 59

Circle the Circle 60
Hoop Relay 61
Quail Shooter's Delight 63
Catch 10 64
Scooter Swing 65
Scooter Slalom 66
Sacky Hack 67
Medley Relay 68
Tree Soccer 68
Bump 68
Blindfold Soccer 69
Tube-e-Cide 70
Pin Ball 72
Outdoor Pin Ball 72
Commandant 73
Whooo 75
Izzat You? 76
Pick & Choose 77
Count Coup 78

Trust **79**
Trust Fall 80
Trust Dive 83
Falling Down Without Going BOOM 85
Spotting 86
Front Roll Practice 86
Back Roll Practice 87
Fall & Roll Exercises 87
Sherpa Walk 89
Yeah, But... 91
Coming and Going of the Rain 92
Squat Thrust 94
Slo-Mo 94

Initiatives **95**
Hog Call 98
Everybody Up 100
Ice Breakers 101
WORDLES 102
All Aboard 106
TT Log 107
Touch My Can 108
Big Business 109
TP Shuffle 110
Group Juggling 112
Ship Wreck 112
Human Ladder 113

Spider Web	114
The Clock	116
Knots	117
Rabid Nugget Rescue	118
Trolley	118
Playpen	120
Traffic Jam	122
2x4	123
Zig Zag	124
Punctured Drum	125
A-Frame	126
Bridge It	127
Macro Tangrams	129
Say What?	130
The Almost Infinite Circle	131
4-Pointer (Monster)	132
Jelly Roll	134
Electric Fence	136
Amazon	137
Diminishing Load	138
Nitro Crossing	139
Soft Walk	140
Mohawk Walk	140
Prouty's Landing	142
I Can Row a Boat...Canoe?	143

Stunts **144**

Snowflake	145
People-to-People Surfing	146
Core Surfing on Foam	146
Paper Core Surfing	146
Surf Massage	146
Balance Practice	147
Orange Teeth	147
Flubber Ball	148
Seat Spin	148
Ten Member Pyramid	149
Mobile 10-Member Pyramid	150
15-Member Pyramid	150
Rope Push	151
Everybody's IT	153
Sore Spot Tag	154
Foetal Tag	154
Hop On Tag	155
Triangle Tag	155
Flip Me the Bird	155
Dizzy Izzy Tag	155

Two in a Row	156
Turnstile	156
Double Dutch	156
Invisible Jump Rope	157
Inchworm	158
Bottoms Up	159
Candle	160
Mini Balance Test	160
Red Baron Stretch	161
5-5-5	161
Stork Stretch	162
Chronological Line-up	163
Balance Broom	164
Hang 10 Climbing Posts	165
Popsicle Push-up	166
Vaulting	167
Dog Shake	168
Funny Face	169
Mirror Image	170
Miniature Monuments	171
P.D.Q.	172
Balloon Blow-up	173
Fried Egg Simulator	174
Dollar Jump	174
Balls Galore	175
Marathon Whistle	175
Lightweight Idea	175
Compass Walk	176
Human Camera	177
Sylvia's Silly Sequence	178
Count Off	179
Medley Relay	179
Mrs. O'Grady	180

PREFACE

Silver Bullets! For many of us, these words conjure up images of masked heroes, of exciting and adventurous chases—perhaps even of Ovaltine shared at radio show time. In that mythic glow of childhood, all things were possible. In play, time itself often stood still while everyone became a little braver, stronger, and more whole. Laughter flowed.

The name, "Silver Bullets," came to Karl and me as we were discussing this book and rambled into nostalgia on our youth. Remember...remember the games...remember the Ovaltine! There was a magic in those times, just as there seems to be a magic in these activities. The thrill of seeing a group of people come together quickly, build trust, begin to solve problems more efficiently—this thrill is reminiscent of early play. In both there is a spirit of playfulness and a flowing of creativity. The most enduring result is a kindred spirit and a feeling of bondedness that transcends words.

The activities of this book have all been used effectively by a variety of teachers, counselors, therapists, camp directors and church leaders. All have wanted an effective, engaging way to bring people together to build trust, and to break down the artificial barriers between individuals and groups of individuals. Karl Rohnke, through his quarterly newsletter, *Bag of Tricks*, maintains a network whereby

graduates of Project Adventure trainings and others can communicate new ideas and activities. Many of this book's ideas have come from that creative networking process.

The benefits of a program that can bring people together are many and growing. The need for such vehicles is being perceived by an increasing number of "people who work with people." It is the main mission of our organization, Project Adventure, Inc., to help schools, agencies, and other institutions realize the benefits of a Project Adventure program. We have taught workshops and constructed challenge courses in all regions of the country.

Our experience with schools and agencies has allowed us to provide a series of model curriculum programs for physical education classes (elementary through college), for counseling groups in a variety of settings, and for interdisciplinary academic classes in middle and secondary schools. The curricula is alive and involving; it is sequenced and adapted by practitioners to meet the needs of each group it serves. As formal curricula, these activities have been evaluated as having improved self-concept, improved the ability of members to take risks, and improved the ability of group members to cooperate and work well together.

Yet we are convinced that the reason for these activities' popularity and effectiveness

cannot really be understood by the results of "valid evaluation." The enduring value is in the magic moments of creativity and good feelings that they can make possible.

So, it matters little whether you remember Ovaltine or not. For whatever age, these "Silver Bullets" can make a difference to your program and the people you work with. Use them in good faith, and enjoy.

By Dick Prouty, Director
Project Adventure, Inc.

FOREWORD

Paolo Friere, the great Brazilian educator, reasoned that nothing has ever been learned without a risk being involved. We can develop this thought into a compelling rationale for risk education.

Learning implies a change state that involves the observation and re-settling processes needed to alter social, behavioural and ecological norms. Uncertainties, frustrations and insecurities will result.

People are at risk when they learn. This risk may be physical, social, emotional, intellectual, or spiritual in nature.

One of the primary objectives of new games, adventure education, initiative tasks, ropes courses, trust activities and inclusive co-operative-competitive games is to help participants deal with the process of risk and the product of behavioural change.

Risk is normal in the daily lives of all human beings and is essential to their education. To avoid the deleterious effects of improperly designed programmes with dangerous consequences, safety is an essential ingredient, but to deny or reduce the risk factor in educational units is to run counter to the educational process itself. Physical educators, recreators, and outdoor specialists have developed certain forms of risk activities designed to inject this essential ingredient into the curriculum. The result has been an in-crease in student motivation, interest, and preparedness to undergo more complex forms of behavioural change. It appears that individuals surround themselves with a "comfort circle," something which prevents them from taking risks or endangering bodily health. This protective factor is essential, of course, but in most people the circle becomes too restrictive, giving rise to boredom, resistance to change, and collective mundanity. People tend not to change jobs or advance in professional endeavors because of this restriction. Whole new forms of recreational activity are denied them because of the "avoidance of risk" syndrome. I would suspect this factor has an uncomfortable influence on the development of self-concept also.

There is little doubt of the value nor the effect of this kind of activity on students; they love it, they search for it, and their wish to participate illustrates clearly that people will respond to challenging, enjoyable and meaningful activity curricula.

The dullness of today's physical education curriculum, so entrapped by traditional sports-oriented skills and lines before endless, outdated apparatus, is capable of repair through the inclusion of activities from the risk curriculum. I commend this movement of which Karl Rohnke is a pioneer and a leader. His work has demonstrated how adventure education can be undertaken in an effective and safe manner.

May he and his colleagues thrive!

By DR. JOHN CHEFFERS
Professor of Education, Boston
    University
Executive Director, Australian
    Institute of Sport

7

Glancing through a local newspaper recently, I was attracted to an article written by a "credentialed" connoisseur of fine restaurants, in which the writer had evaluated local eateries she frequented using a five star grading system. (I'm a sucker for here's-what-I-think articles, particularly if the author uses stars. I suppose because it gives the reader a chance to either justify a personal choice or strongly disagree without fear of retaliation.) This particular gourmet stated that she liked **all** *the restaurants that were included; so, using the five-star system, she graded no restaurant lower than 3 stars, explaining that 2-½ (**½) was her grade for "good."*

The three-star method I have used to rate almost each game, stunt, or event in this book is also a bit superfluous in that I wouldn't have included the activity unless I thought it was fun, functional and reasonably safe. But, I can't resist letting you know which have been my favorites over the years; and I also want to indicate the newer activities that seem to have a potential for high use. So: *good; ** better; *** best. Experienced players, please disagree with any subjective choice or rating—that's part of the game.

Raison d'etre

Notwithstanding stars and humor, the purpose of this game, stunt, and initiative problem collection is to provide you with proven educational tools that do what they are designed to do. The skill demonstrated in the use of a tool in construction or education is, of course, a function of the user's ability and experience. But, be of good cheer; initiative problems and adventure games are user-friendly and well received by almost everyone.

The following chapters offer those tools that have proven over the years to be the most valuable; i.e., they work and people like them. Initiative problems and adventure games and New Games and ASE's and all activities of that get-to-know-you; get-to-know-yourself; have fun; be challenged; take-a-risk; get scared; cooperate; share; fail; or succeed genre have been collected and written about in a number of recent publications and less formal printings. But the content of these anthologies have been somewhat predictable in content. . .isn't there anything beyond the Electric Fence? If you don't know what I'm alluding to, the contents of this book should be pure discovery: enjoy! But, for you game-jaded fizz-ed folks and recreation leaders who have done the Lap Game 137 times, here's relief.

Inventing a playable game or a workable initiative pro-

blem is more difficult than most people realize, and coming up with an enjoyable, playable game is tougher yet. So, if someone responds to your lack-of-ideas complaint by suggesting that you "use your imagination," refer to Rohnke's expurgated collection of some old, some new, some borrowed, and some plagiarized curriculum ideas.

My personal experiences with these types of activities began in the military, continued and became more humane as an instructor for Outward Bound, and have since further mellowed and expanded as a Project Adventure, Inc. employee. Notwithstanding the organization, the situation has always been that when a group needed a morale boost or a means of gaining behaviorial insights, a well-chosen game or initiative problem was a surefire and enjoyable way to accomplish that goal.

LEARNING GOALS

Much of the rationale and justification for an "adventure approach" emerges out of an individual's experience in trying an activity. There are, however, some important goals (not immediately evident from reading or participating) that are at the very heart of programmatic adventure, tying together all the varied activities. These learning goals are:

1. *TO INCREASE THE PARTICIPANT'S SENSE OF PERSONAL CONFIDENCE. The aim of many activities is to allow people to view themselves as increasingly capable and competent. By attempting a graduated series of activities which involve physical or emotional risk, and succeeding (or sometimes failing) in a supportive group atmosphere, a person may begin to develop true self-esteem.*

2. *TO INCREASE MUTUAL SUPPORT WITHIN A GROUP. The assumption is that anyone who conscientiously tries should be respected. Success and failure are less important than making an effort. In many cases, the success or failure of a group depends on the effort of the members. A cooperative, supportive atmosphere tends to encourage participation.*

3. *TO DEVELOP AN INCREASED LEVEL OF AGILITY AND PHYSICAL COORDINATION. A number of exercises and games entail the use of balance and smoothly flowing movement. Balance and coordinated movement form the basis for many physical activities ranging from dancing to track and football. People who perceive themselves as physically awkward often see themselves as inadequate in other ways. Balance, coordination and agility can be improved by practice. Such improvement often generates a feeling of personal worth well beyond the tangible accomplishment.*

4. *TO DEVELOP AN INCREASED JOY IN ONE'S PHYSICAL SELF AND IN BEING WITH OTHERS. One of the criteria used in assessing various activities is that **it must have an element of fun in it.** Instructors are not solemnly engaged in building confidence, social cohesion and agility. Just as people approaching new situations may be anxious and even fearful, so should they experience joy, laughter, anticipation.*

9

Organization of this book

All the activities are included under the following chapter headings:

Games • Stunts • Initiative Problems • Trust Activities

Whether you can use a particular game, initiative problem or stunt might depend upon the space needed, materials at hand and the activity level planned for the group. To help you choose an appropriate activity I've incorporated a few symbols next to each title (after the stars) that will help identify what the activity's limitations are and what it has to offer.

10

 - an outside activity

 - an indoor activity

 - can be accomplished as well as either indoor/outdoor

 - activity level high (includes considerable movement or running)

 - activity level not so high (no perspiration or hard breathing)

 - needs props of some kind

- no props necessary — people only

Before you start gaming and facilitating, here's a foreshortened adventure education formula that is the distillation of many years experience with educating and training people; age and location notwithstanding.

The essence of this formula (no panacea intended) deals with so many educational and psychological theories, opinions, jargon, and programmed confusers that I have probably oversimplified in hopes of demystifying a potentially complex approach. I have written it as I try to remember it.

1. NO TRUST — NO BEGINNING
2. NO FUN — NO RETURN (of students)
3. NO CHALLENGE — NO CONTINUATION

1. If your students don't trust you; your purpose; their peers; the approach; program time will be limited to hassles, bickering, reluctance, and a huge waste of time.

The activities in this book engender trust — you need it.

2. If you are so into the seriousness of educating that the essential fun inherent in learning has been squeezed out, then "by-the-numbers" is in. Rote learning is OK for multiplication tables, but there's certainly more joy in learning than 7 x 9 = 63 provides.

The activities in this book have fun in mind — it's essential.

3. If what you are doing is so geared to successful completion that failure is nonexistent, then boredom replaces challenge.

Understandable stress and commitment to challenge are woven throughout the activities in this book — you gotta have it.

Ye Olde Basic Disclaimer and Safety Reminder

Hey, don't look at me!

Reasonable risk-taking is part of living. The reasonable risks present in this anthology of games and activities that could result in emotional upset or physical harm can be minimized by operating within the parameters of a programmed adventure approach; i.e., knowing what the results will be of whatever adventure you are promoting. Let the "perceived risk" remain (it's a valuable teaching tool), but operate, on a day-to-day basis, utilizing proven safety procedures for predictable results.

If you and others are free-associating with possible adventure activity ideas for curriculum use, contemplate closely the possible consequences of your new plan and then put your safety or ego on the line before you ask students or other clientele to try the activity. "Calculated abandon" is an OK approach as long as the calculations are well done and tested.

In keeping with these BE CAREFUL chidings, be advised that Karl Rohnke and Project Adventure, Inc., cannot and do not assume responsibility or liability for the use of information offered in this book—written or implied.

Operate with gusto, tempered with experienced hindsight and the happy suspicion that there will be a tomorrow.

READ THIS FIRST —
(or the limited literary warranty is not valid)

The intent of collecting and organizing all these activities and fun-filled folderol is not to facilitate lesson planning for physical education teachers (First Day—pg. 17; Second Day—pg. 87, etc.). Any interested individual working with people in a variety of settings can use these ideas and schemes to encourage participation and learning in a way that is immediate, involving, and enjoyable. Teachers, parents, recreation leaders, mental health clinicians, summer camp counselors, church workers—this material is for you.

This anthology of over 160 activities also fulfills a more program-oriented purpose representing the ground level curriculum of the Project Adventure physical education program and also a large part of the Adventure-Based Counseling (ABC) approach. Now, when workshop participants ask, "Isn't all this material written down somewhere?", the answer is yes; at least for the next couple of weeks until the next great game or idea unfolds.

Photo by—PETER STEELE

13

INTRODUCTION TO GAMES SECTION

I have tried to make this collection of games as fresh and unique as possible. If there is a game in here that you recognize from another book, it's because I found the activity to be so outstanding that I don't want you to miss it.

A game can be an end in itself. I have no doubt, from having played many games as an adult, that the justification for participating in game activities can be for personal enjoyment only. Notice the period at the end of the last sentence. That's it—that's the reason—period. No validity hassles; or attempting to manipulate the cognitive, affective, psychomotor triumverate—just flat-out fun.

If your ongoing program needs a boost because of scheduling problems, personality conflicts or activity repetition, try playing a couple of these games. Games, presented in a lighthearted manner, can provide the morale growth that facilitates group cohesion and enthusiasm for the program. De-emphasize competition and try to present the activities in such an attractive way that everyone will want to participate. It's hard to turn your back on obvious fun.

Play Pointers:
1. Don't just explain; involve yourself in the activity. You don't have to play every game, but be ready to personalize the game with your person; get in there and mix it up with the players.
2. Keep the rules to a minimum. Wordy explanations lead to pre-game boredom.
3. Bend some rules occasionally or change a few as fits the players and the situations.

4. Don't run a good game into the ground. Three straight class periods of any game in this section is boring. That's why some students don't like archery or badminton or anything that is required too many weeks in a row.
5. Keep the players playing. Don't include or evolve rules that permanently eliminate participants.
6. Pick teams that are fair. Don't use the disastrous sociogram method for choosing sides; i.e., asking two students to pick their own teams.
7. Play games that allow as much of a 50/50 male-female split as possible. Organized sports generally demand a sex split and there's enough of that. These games can be played as well by either sex.
8. Emphasize competition against self when competition seems natural. Trying to beat a time established by your own team or attempting to smash a nebulous WORLD RECORD is great fun with none of the second place, next time symptoms of the loser syndrome.

Toss-A-Name Game***

If you have trouble remembering a bunch of new names in a just-met group situation and you dislike name tags, (Hello, my name is _____) as much as I do, this game provides an action-packed sequence that makes forgetting harder than remembering.

Break up into groups of about 8-10 people, and stand in an informal circle (no holding hands or dress-right-dress is necessary). A leader introduces the game by saying his/her first name, then tosses a tennis ball (or whatever) to the person on his/her right or left. Continuing in one direction, each person says his/her first name and continues tossing the ball in sequence until the leader again has the ball. The leader then calls out someone's name in the circle (You do have to remember at least one person's name!) and lofts the ball to her/him, and that person calls another individual's name, etc., etc.

After the ball has been flying about for a few minutes, or more usefully after you begin to get a feel for all the names in the group, start up another ball, increasing the frequency of names being called and the action. Add a third ball toward the end of the game just for fun, because at this point the law of diminishing returns creeps in. Names and balls are flying about so rapidly that it's hard to pinpoint who's who as balls career off heads and bodies.

If there are other groups playing the same game, stop occasionally and ask a third of the group (3 groups) to transfer to another group and begin the action again. After awhile announce to the three groups that anyone can change groups whenever he/she wants to, ensuring that everyone gets to hear each person's name.

Name Games Variations:

1. Standing in a circle, begin moving slowly away from one another, but continue tossing the nuggets and calling names. The farther apart you get, the louder you have to shout the names and the more you have to *loft* the ball. Slowly begin moving closer (balls and names continue) until the group is so close together that the game dissolves into laughter. For this contracting/expanding variation, have at least one ball per three people in use; i.e., 30 people—10 balls.

2. After the names begin to flow, and as a means of reinforcement, ask the catcher to say thank you to the thrower, including the thrower's name.

3. As a finale, bring the whole group together (nuggets set aside) and ask if there is anyone who can name everyone. In a group of 25, you should get 3-6 volunteers, and the person you choose will usually be 100% correct in his/her attempt. It's an impressive and predictable feat.

4. Then indicate that the activity will end with a cocktail party. Assume and demonstrate the proper position and air of self-assurance (one arm bent holding an imaginary cocktail; the other hand ready to shake hands), and commence mingling. At this point, you step to the person nearest you (if you remember his/her name) and say cheerily (big smile), "Glad you could make it Doug" (or Whomever) while shaking his/her hand. Move quickly to the next person and so on. Include a hug occasionally, but be careful not to spill your drink. Invite the group to join your conviviality, explaining that it's their party. This name-sharing encounter usually continues for a minute or so and gradually subsides into spontaneous individual conversations. Nice going—you have facilitated.

17

Here is a unique game that requires little skill, includes any amount of people and is 100% active. The object of play is for a group of any size to keep an equal number of assigned tennis balls moving about a gymnasium floor until six penalties have been indicated by the referee.

The game vocabulary, which is the key to contemporary tradition, goes like this:

Rabid Nugget—a moving tennis ball
Hectic—a stationary tennis ball
Berserk—a referee's scream, designating a penalty
Frenzy—an elapsed time period measuring six Berserks
Logic—a tennis ball that becomes lodged unintentionally on or behind something
Illogic—a tennis ball that is craftily stuck on or behind something
Paranoia—a player's feeling that the refs are picking on her/him

Rules and Use of Terminology

If thirty players are on the gym floor, thirty *Rabid Nuggets* are thrown, rolled, kicked, or bounced simultaneously onto the floor by one of the refs to initiate the game and start the timing. There are three referees; one at each end of the court and one off to the side at midcourt. It is the duty of the two refs on the floor to try and spot *Hectics* and to generate a hysterical *Berserk* (scream) so that all will recognize a penalty. The group has five seconds to start a *Hectic* moving again or another full-throated *Beserk* is issued. The Berserking ref must point condemningly at the *Hectic* until it is again provided impetus.

Every fifteen seconds after a start, the side line ref puts an additional *Rabid Nugget* into play until the final *Berserk* has been recorded. The team is allowed six *Berserks*, at which juncture the ref on the side line, who is responsible for timing this melee, jumps up and down waving his arms, yelling STOP—STOP—STOP.

The team intent is to keep the *Rabid Nuggets* moving as long as possible before six *Berserks* have been recorded. This time span is called a *Frenzy*. After a *Frenzy*, ask the group to talk about and develop a strategy in order to keep the *Rabid Nuggets* moving for a longer span of time; i.e., increasing the duration of the *Frenzy*.

Rule Refinements for Frantic Freaks

A *Rabid Nugget* must be kicked (only kicked) randomly or to another player. It may not be held underfoot and simply moved back and forth. This rule was recently included to counter the basically sneaky player who's always looking for a way around the rules in the guise of initiative.

If a *Rabid Nugget* becomes a *Logic* or *Illogic*, the ref must get the nugget back into motion. An illogic receives an immediate berserk.

Official optic yellow USLTA tennis balls are not essential to achieve satisfying play. The short game version involves using bowling balls or helium-filled balloons.

18

Balloon Frantic **

Rabid Nugget Redux

Substitute balloons for old tennis balls, and you have *Balloon Frantic.* This lofty game is best played indoors in a high ceiling gymnasium or outdoors on a windless day.

Ask each participant to blow up a balloon to about 12 in. diameter size. Don't use so-called "penny balloons" as they are too small when expanded and don't result in satisfying play. Inflate at least 6-8 extra balloons to serve as throw-ins for the 15 second rule, or as replacements for the inevitable broken balloon (boomers).

The basic rules for both games are identical except for the start. Ask each player to throw their balloon into the air, rather than having the referee start things with a kick, as in the basic *Frantic.*

Be sure to have a camera available to record this game on film, because the technicolor action is poster material.

Here are two more tennis ball games to further justify retiring more of those dead fuzzies that aren't responding to your devastating top spin shot.

But first, a preliminary bit of information about using paper cores. (Hold onto those balls over there, or I'll have to collect them!) Paper cores are the discarded center sections of industrial rolls of paper. These substantial cardboard cylinders measure about 3 feet long and have a diameter of approximately 16 inches. The best part about them is that they are free — usually. Try to find an industrial paper producer in a city near you and ask for the core discards; companies are often glad to get rid of them. Take a station wagon or pickup truck and load up, as there are all kinds of adventure curriculum uses for these multi-purpose cylinders. The reason I've written all this core material information (while you're standing there fiddling with your tennis balls) is that the cores are integral parts of the following activities.

On a flat uniform surface see how many cores can be stacked on top of one another to form a column; no props allowed, just people. The record number of cores is more than you would initially believe, and probably higher than you want or need to go.

Caution — if the column begins to fall (watch the top) during the stacking process, let it go! Trying to catch the tumbling cores is unnecessary and dangerous. The falling cores will not damage the gym floor.

You will need a completed column (7-8 cores for the game *Paul's Balls,* but if you feel like knocking the stack down (How can you resist?) give participants a tennis ball or three and see if they can knock off one core at a time by throwing the balls at the top core. You can also suggest a group blow. It won't work, but it's interesting to see thirty people trying to blow over a huge jointed paper column.

20

2. Paul's Balls ***

This active, minimum skill activity was named after its originator, Paul somebody-or-other. If his name had been Fred, we would have had to think up another name.

Each person has one tennis ball. The object is to see how long it takes the group to put all the balls into the core column by lofting them up and in. The column should be about 7-8 stacked cores high in order to produce a substantial group challenge. It's interesting to witness and hard to explain how engrossing and enjoyable this simple task can be. Time how long it takes for the group to "sink" all the balls. After a brief strategy session, time a second attempt and see if the group has learned anything about cooperation as a result of the first attempt.

How do you get all the balls out? I'm sure you and your students can find a way. If you have Hula Hoops available, an alternate game is to see how long it takes the group to toss all the hoops up and over the column. The name of the game is, of course, Helga's Hoops.

A Safe Stack

If the idea of stacking paper cores to a height of 8 or more is distressing from a safety standpoint, or if obtaining the paper cores has proved difficult, try stacking firmly inflated automobile inner tubes. If the stack falls over in mid-attempt, there is minimized danger of injury — falling inner tubes don't dent heads.

You may experience some problems using inner tubes and one is finding them, as most auto tires are now tubeless. Another hassle is storage (you will need about 25-30 tubes for a world class effort) unless you plan to deflate the tubes each time. However, if this deflation idea makes sense, your time priorities may be out of sync with the world.

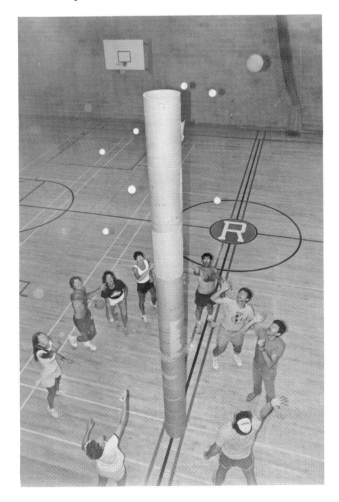

Tattoo**

It's hard to appreciate the use or enjoyment of this multi-ball activity unless you become involved. The name of the game might as well be, *"What am I doing?"* The activity satisfies a need for movement, accomplishment and personal satisfaction in addition to being more totally kinetic and visual than any other group activity I can think of (besides rock'n roll).

Give each participant (10-50 people) 3-4 rabid nuggets (tennis balls) and ask the players to arrange themselves behind the mid-line of an indoor basketball court; facing toward one of the backboards. (For this throwing sequence to work, there must be a wall behind the backboard; i.e. not bleachers.)

Indicate that on GO, they are to aim and throw their hardest so the nuggets hit the backboard and to continue throwing, attempting to produce a drum-like "tattoo" sound on the backboard. After firing their initial nuggets, they must nab a rebounding ball or two and continue their assault.

All the nuggets will not rebound back to the throwers, so a couple of volunteers must position themselves somewhere under the backboard to retrieve stray projectiles. Being a retriever is not as crazy as it sounds, since all the throwers are aiming well over the downcourt volunteers' heads. A ricochet might bounce off one's head or body, but the action potential and minor consequences make the "under fire" position more attractive.

Let the "fire-at-will" action continue for at least a minute. The sound and movement are rewards in themselves. In addition: 1) Those people who like to throw and throw well can "chuck" as many balls as hard as they want to and cheer their own efforts and accuracy (because no one else is paying attention to them or can tell who's throwing what where). 2) Those folks who can't throw well can either throw a few nuggets or none at all without fear of censure, because (as above) nobody's watching *their* efforts.

After things slow down a bit, ask each person to retrieve and hold 2 or 3 nuggets. Indicate that you want to start the same activity but this time by throwing with the opposite arm. The results are humbling and humorous. Almost everyone does poorly, except the ambidextrous few, so reluctance to try is quickly put aside. After 30 seconds of high arced and poorly aimed throws (and much good-natured ribbing), let them finish up with a few *good hard ones* by signaling them to return to their natural throwing arm.

Nugget Alternatives:

1. Ask a nuggeted group, standing at one end of the basketball court (backs against the wall) if they can hit the far wall with a ball thrown by their "opposite" arm. After a few attempts (some success, some not), let them finish up with a few throws with their "good" arm. You will be surprised at how many good athletes cannot throw a ball the length of a basketball court with their "non throwing" arm.

2. Request that everyone pair up for the next activity, the "Howitzer Throw." The object of this command/response bit of cooperation is to have one participant tell his/her blindfolded (eyes closed) partner where to throw a ball in order to hit a target (backboard, championship pennant, buzzer, etc.). The partners may not touch one another; only words of direction are allowed. Six shots at one target are delivered and then another target is chosen. People should not become target material. Switch roles after a few attempts.

22

Mine Field**

Scatter your collection of rabid nuggets (tennis balls) onto a floor area and arrange them so that they are randomly but somewhat equally distributed within and about the available area of play. About 300-500 balls are required for a typical mine field arrangement.

The object of this highly visual activity is to verbally guide a blindfolded partner through the mine field to the far safe side. Verbal directions must come from the sidelines; i.e., the verbal leader is not allowed to stand next to his/her partner within the mine field.

The soft-footed jaunt from boundary to boundary is timed. For each nugget touched there is a 15 sec. time penalty added to the final time. Have each pair trade roles after an initial attempt.

For intense alternative action try the pursuit variable of releasing a heat seeking missile (HSM).

In this game action the blindfolder player (as above) is called The Sidewinder, a highly accurate and devastatingly destructive missile. The Sidewinder is aimed at a target on the far side of the room (chair, table, etc.) and is set in motion by the person giving step-by-step instructions. If the Sidewinder touches a tennis ball enroute he/she must swing both of their arms in a full circle 15 times, counting aloud each revolution.

Sixty seconds after the Sidewinder is launched an antimissile missile is also launched. The second blindfolded player represents a heat seeking missile and is trying to destroy (tag) the Sidewinder before the target is reached. If the HSM touches a nugget, he/she must bend over and touch their toes (ankles, knees, whatever) 10 times, counting each repetition aloud.

Filling the floor with Sidewinders and HSM's provides a military melee of more than modest proportions. Great fun for all, warhead affiliation notwithstanding.

Where the Balls Are

It soon becomes obvious that to properly offer the preceding tennis ball activities, you need "beaucoup" balls. From past experience, the following sources for used balls are worthwhile pursuing.

BEST — Make a deal with a tennis club or pro to barter or buy their used balls. Tennis facilities use an inordinate amount (hundreds) of balls, retiring them after only a few sets. Tell the owner that the balls are to be used in an educational program and are not to be recycled for proletarian court play. (Non-profit organizations and schools may allow a donor to take a charitable deduction at tax time).

NOT BAD, BUT SEASONAL — Check the rooftops of a school's gymnasium. Gym roofs are invariably flat (that's why they always leak), and they eat tennis balls (and shoes, locks, golf balls, etc.).

POOR, BUT GOOD FOR A FEW — Stand around a municipal tennis court and sneak off with out-of-bound balls. Be fair though— let the ball come to a stop before you claim it.

Physics Phantasy**

Old socks, weighted with sand or rocks, have been thown around by kids for years and years; even I remember doing it. The New Games Foundation popularized this spontaneous fun by replacing the sand (which doubled as a weapon) with a nerf ball and calling the centrifugal device a something-or-other; it's a whimsical name that I can't recall. (Did the old spinning sock have a name when you were a kid? I can't seem to remember ever calling it anything but a "rock sock"; a sobriquet that mothers and homeowners near my turf learned to hate.)

Try playing catch with a sand-weighted sock. Keep moving apart as you become more adept at throwing and catching. See which pair of throwers on a football field can move the farthest apart and make a dual catch.

If you don't have any sand around for filling the sock, try inserting a tennis ball or a nerf ball. Don't catch the weighted end, but try and snatch the flapping tail—much more aesthetic and skill oriented. The first few tries at throwing for distance are usually wildly inaccurate, and dangerous if you are standing too near the thrower (nerfball excluded). A discus-like spin produces the farthest and most errant throws; some tosses head straight up or backwards. Some throwers, into the zen of existential sand socks, feel there is no backwards if you don't care where the thrown implement is going. Watch out for these guys!

Comet Ball Horseshoes**

Use two hula hoops or inflated bicycle inner tubes as targets and place them approximately 25 yards apart. Use sand-filled socks as horseshoes and play regulation horseshoe rules using this suggested scoring system:

10 pts. - sock completely inside the tube or hoop
5 pts. - sock touching the tube or hoop
2 pts. - 6" away
1 pt. - up to 12"
12" or more away — forget it!

Ultimate Comet Ball*

Yep, you guessed it—right from the world of Wham-O. Rules duplicate those of Ultimate Frisbee. The behind-the-back shot is an absolutely classic move with a weighted sock, and notwithstanding the aesthetic qualities and form-pleasing characteristics, it should be outlawed because of sock/jock contact with resultant diminished desire to continue play.

Before leaving the world of socks, a few suggestions: 1) If possible, use long socks (much better flight characteristics and centrifugal leverage). 2) Make sure the socks are one of a kind or well used; to maintain marital or family peace. 3) Fill the socks with flour and have bludgeon-each-other contests (no head shots, please).

25

I think this game is unique. I have tried only pieces of it as part of another game, but its potential is worth developing—the action and reactions are fast and well received. The following paragraphs introduce the two objects of play and offers an outline of game possibilites.

Mirrors

These surrogate laser reflectors can vary in size from the small purse mirror type to as large as you can afford or attempt to carry. The mirror serves as a game weapon. If reflected sunlight (flash) is seen by an opposing player, that player is frozen temporarily (movement from the immediate area is restricted for 2 minutes). A small mirror is easy to carry but is hard to aim accurately. A larger mirror, say 10" x 12", reflects considerably more light and is easier to aim because of the more visible light beam. As it hits various objects there is no doubt whether you have been zapped by a mirror; the reflected glint of the sun sets off a retinal alarm that's hard to ignore.

A pre-game joint decision that adds to the game's enjoyment is the agreement that all players hit by a light flash must punctuate their retinal trauma by falling down and simultaneously yelling, thus indicating to the light wielder that he/she has scored. Picking off a player from 200-300 yards distance is undeniably fun and strategically useful.

Various ploys can be used to counteract the flash. 1) Don't look at a player who is trying to flash you. 2) Wear a set of goggles (we call this prop, the *Goggles of RA*) that are somehow woven into the game to provide immunity from the mirror's devastation. 3) Try reflecting the sun back at the person initiating the flash: called the Quid Pro Quo Flash or QPQF (pronounced simply, Cue Pee to knowledgeable players). 4) Try to maintain as much of a "downsun" position as possible. Be careful though, a large mirror is capable of reflecting 360°, depending upon the sun's position in the sky.

Mirrors and Mortars**

Mortars

A mortar is represented by a long sock with 2 or 3 tennis balls dropped in. Long sports tube socks work well, but panty hose drawn and quartered are better. Plop in the balls and tie off the open ends with an overhand knot.

The sock mortar is used as a weapon by throwing it much as a mortar is projected; in a long parabolic arc. The rules concerning such a throw are: a) The mortar, to be effective, must land within 10 feet of the opposing player. b) The mortar must achieve at least a 10 feet apogee (height) to be armed. c) All players (including the thrower) within the 10 feet diameter devastation zone are "frozen" for two minutes.

If the mortar's tail is caught during its descent by the proposed victim, the thrower and anyone within 10 feet of him/her are frozen for three minutes.

Long-arcing throws (40 yds. or more) are possible by twirling the sock (discus fashion) before letting go. If 3 players join hands they become a "tank" and are invulnerable to mortar shots.

Ultimately, there should be some definable reason for all this flashing and twirling; perhaps a team competition of sorts? Pattern it after the game, *Capture the Flag,* where each team seeks a particular object and must take the retrieved talisman to a winning area. To extend the length of a game, use two retrievable objects.

The obvious limitation to this game is the need for sunshine. A perfectly clear day is not necessary, however, because intermittent clouds add a different twist to the game; reducing the power of the light wielders. If it's an absolutely gray day — stay home; who needs it?

Admittedly, the above rules are not in logical order and the context is a bit shaky, but here's your chance to make up your own rules. We have used the socks and mirrors successfully as part of another game, so I know they work as "weapons": fun to use and fun to avoid.

Fast Draw*

Since you already have a number of small pocket mirrors around for use in the preceding game, try this fast action one-on-one confrontation.

Hold the mirror on your hip, as if you were reaching for a six-gun. In a paired-off situation, with the potential Wyatt Earps standing about 10 yards apart, you are ready for a showdown. The first fast-draw artist to hit his/her opponent's retinal area with a flash is the winner. Play again, or challenge the champion. Note the opportunity for inventive role-playing.

When two people face off, the sun must be situated so that each player has approximately the same light angle to use, otherwise one player has a distinct advantage. Skewing the angle might not be a bad idea to develop parity amongst combatants.

Have the pairs stand farther apart to offer a more difficult target. There should be no doubt in the players' minds when they have been flashed.

If the thought of "gunfighting" does not appeal, have the two flashers face "up-sun" toward a shaded wall. Using an agreed-upon target on the wall, these fast draw contests can be considerably less sanguinary.

Think of team contests although team affiliation isn't the appropriate word in this case—think. . .family (the Earps, Dalton Brothers); or gang (Jessie James', Hole-in-the-Wall Gang, etc.). Picture groups of mirror wielders trying to "wipe-out" the opposing flashers. Such a contest could begin in an open field and spill over to a wooded or building area. Have you ever been flashed from behind a Shag Bark Hickory?

Off the Wall (Indoor Frisbee Game)**

This atypical frisbee game (is there such a thing?) is an elitist variation of the old GUTS model. This is not a game for everyone, because some skill in throwing and catching a frisbee is required. But wait—let me explain the rules quickly before you skip this game and miss out on some off-the-wall fun.

Arrange and disperse 6-8 people at each end of a vacant gym. As in GUTS a frisbee is thrown back and forth with the attempt to make the other team miss (drop the frisbee). The major rule change here is that the frisbee may hit the back or side walls (or any other obstacle that can be aimed at: a backboard, for example).

1. Ceiling shots result in a "no throw"—neither team adds or subtracts a point. (The reason for this rule is that many ceilings are "soft" or are of the drop ceiling variety so that hard frisbee throws can cause property damage and hassles with the custodians.)
2. Short thows (short of the catchers) also result in a "no throw" situation.
3. The frisbee must approach the defenders between a 45° and horizontal level, or a "no throw" results.
4. Impossible-to-reach shots are judged individually and result in some memorable arguments.
5. Skip shots are allowed if the frisbee reaches the defenders at a minimum of waist height.
6. Only one-hand catches are allowed unless the decision of both teams is to make the game easier, then two-hand catches are OK.
7. Tip or rebound catches (from player to player) are OK, and in a heated contest programmed fumbles can be spectacular.
8. No "flying missile," knock-off-your-fingernail shots are allowed. However, direct shots are acceptable; i.e., not off-the-wall.
9. Your team can receive multiple points if the frisbee hits more than one object. If a saucer hits two walls and a backboard, 3 points are awarded for that throw *if* the throw is dropped.

Off the Wall is a fine game for the talented frisbee thrower, but its drawbacks include:

1. At least a moderate skill level is required to enjoy the game.
2. Only a comparatively small number can play.
3. An entire gym is needed to play.

Frisbee Shuffleboard*

Since you have taken over the gym for a game of *Off the Wall,* try this airborne variation of shuffleboard.

As in shuffleboard or horseshoes, two players compete against two other players. The object is to throw your team's frisbees (3-5) into the key (circular) area at one end of the gym from the far end of the gym. Throwers stand just beyond the out-of-bounds line under the basketball backboard.

The key is divided into three areas. The closest (and smallest) area is worth 3 points. The next area scores 2 points and the far area 1 point. If the frisbee is touching any line, no points are scored.

Smooth, low, gliding (on the floor) throws work best. With additional practice, it's possible to knock an opponent's frisbee out of a scoring area, or into one. Each team must use different color frisbees to avoid scoring confusion. Softies (flexible saucers) work well for this game also.

Sardines**

I was introduced to this hide-and-go-seek game by the participants in an adventure workshop in North Carolina. The game works best in an area that has lots of nooks and crannies (of ample size) to jam lots of bodies into. An open gymnasium is not a good choice. The game is best played at night indoors in a large multi-story building.

The Game

Traditionally, the person designated as IT in a hide-and-seek game should count to 100 with eyes closed while everyone else hides ..."97, 98, 99, 100...anybody around my base is IT." However, in this game, the IT hides and everyone else tries to find the hidden IT.

As the seeking folks wander about, poking into closets or behind doors, they should be aware that if they spot the IT person, they must join IT in hiding by sharing the hiding place (thus the name Sardines).

The game continues until everyone has found everyone and the seekers become one group with IT.

This is NOT a game to build trust, as you must be fairly sneaky to join the IT without being seen by the other seekers. For example, "Sue, you go down the hall and I'll go this way"—knowing full well that "this way" is to join the hiding IT, while Sue seeks the wild goose.

A Classic Game Vignette:

A memorable Sardine game of recent years, during which I was the hider (IT) allowed me to pick an ideal corner in a dark room as a hiding spot. I was absolutely invisible in that corner and no one had found me 20 minutes into the game.

I was sitting motionless with my knees tucked up next to my chest as a tenacious female hunter came into my room for the third time and announced to the dark that she knew I had to be in this room. I could see her outline against a window as she slowly made her way toward my position; hands outstretched, feeling for the Sardine she ESP'd was near.

As her groping hand neared, I leaned my head back as far as I could so that I was then looking at the ceiling. Sensing that she was near, her probing hand movements quickened and one of her exploring digits entered one of my well-positioned nostrils. End of story. End of game.

Moonball**

Moonball is an excellent one-prop-game that develops cooperation and fast reactions. Play becomes intensely competitive, as a group competes against its last best effort.

Scatter your group (any number, but use 2 or more balls as the group size demands) on a basketball court or a field. Use a well inflated beach ball as the object of play. The group's objective is to hit the ball aloft as many times as possible before the ball strikes the ground.

Rules: (1) A player cannot hit the ball twice in succession.
(2) Count one point for each hit.

Not too complicated, eh?

The tension and expectation builds as each "world record" is approached. Moonball is popular with all ages because it's simple to understand, requires little skill and involves (like it or not) everyone.

Do not use a volleyball, basketball, etc., for this game. A beach ball is a non-intimidating, fun-related object of play and its flight characteristics fit in well with the low-key emphasis.

31

Paper Golf**

Whacking a golf ball around the links is a comparatively unphysical means of spending exercise time, from a cardio-vascular standpoint. I'd like to further reduce your oxygen uptake by introducing you to Paper Golf, a fiendishly clever, intriguing, and fascinating paper and pencil game of golf.

You will need 18 sheets of unlined paper. The size of the paper is up to you, but generally the larger the paper, the more demanding (not physically) the game becomes.

Refer to the illustration for a typical Paper Golf hole set-up. Your imagination and golf experience will allow you to make up the other 17 holes on separate sheets. Imagination counts for more than artistic ability.

The game is best played by a foursome (that's golf talk for 4 players playing a round [9 or 18 holes] together), but can be played by any number; i.e., until the pen or pencil lines become confusingly intertwined. Use a different colored pen or pencil for each player.

To Play

Golfer number one places the point of his/her pencil/pen directly on the paper anywhere between the two markers designating the tee. (It quickly becomes obvious that this paper game of golf uses the same vocabulary and rules extant in regulation golf, and as such, provides an enjoyable method of learning the basic vocabulary of the game without suffering the frustrations of "keeping your head down," "maintaining a stiff left arm," "controlling the back swing," etc.

The player eyeballs the distance from tee to green, recognizing the added stroke obstacles that will increase the score, and plans a first stroke (drive) that will place the ball (tip of the pen) in a safe "well hit" area of the fairway.

After the player has planned his drive, he must *close his eyes* and keep them closed for 5 seconds before moving the pen. Only one continuous move (straight or curving) may be executed. When the pen tip stops, the ball stops. If the pen tip ends up in the bunker or hazard, appropriate penalty strokes are added to the score.

The player must then plan the next stroke (with eyes open) and execute the stroke (eyes closed) toward the pin (hole). To finish the hole, the pen tip must end up directly in the open area of the hole.

As you develop each hole on separate pieces of paper, use your imagination to vary the obstacles and distance and thus the par value for each hole. Remember the old putting adage, "never up, never in," and on the next hole "let out a little shaft."

32

Paper Links Golf Club
Hole #18
Par 3

Which Way? Softball*

Trying to referee this game can be as confusing as trying to follow the rules. Better reproduce the rules on your palm for a quick reference. If confused, you can pretend you're checking a blister or splinter or something. . . Where a player runs after hitting the ball, in ordinary softball, is predictable, but by radically changing the base-running rules, a 12-week semester, everyday ho-hum game can become a physical *and* intellectual challenge.

1st inning - run the bases in reverse
2nd inning - 2nd base becomes 1st base - 1st becomes 3rd
3rd inning - When the ball is hit to the right side of the field (or infield), the player runs to 3rd base first and proceeds around the bases in reverse. If the next batter hits the ball to the left side of the field, then the players run to 1st base. If the players are on base, they must determine which is the correct direction to run based on where the ball is hit.

Remember ref, the decisions are up to you. It gets easier after the first semester!

Bob Nilson

Impulse**

This lightning-fast, hand-holding game is suitable for practically any age level, and particularly for a group that likes to compete against itself.

Ask your group to form a hand-in-hand circle around you. A larger group will observe more hand action taking place as the impulse travels the circle than a smaller group will—say 30 versus 10. Go for a larger group.

Using a stopwatch (can you believe those inexpensive electronic LCD watches? —flashing rapid-fire numbers from who knows where, and accurate to 1/100 of a second. Functional and oozing mystique—what a deal!), time how long it takes to send a hand-squeezed impulse around the circle. Ask an individual in the circle to start and stop the impulse, saying GO and, eventually, STOP when the impulse returns to the opposite hand.

Repeat the attempt a number of times to see how much the group can improve their speed (cooperation, physical reaction, anticipation, efficiency). Vary the activity by trying the same thing with everyone's eyes closed, and compare times with the eyes-open attempts. Additionally, ask the initiator to start the impulse going in both directions at once by squeezing his/her right and left hands simultaneously. See if the head-on impulses can pass through one another, or if they get lost at a hand-held juncture; usually a pair of confused and twitching participants.

Circle-centered impulses can be passed in a variety of other ways. Slaps, bumps, smacks, whistles, blows—this can be a very intense experience. Experiment! Try lying down in a circle—foot-to-hand!

Body English*

A group tries to spell out the words to a well known proverb by using their bodies as letters. (Forming letters with the fingers is not allowed — too easy.) Another group tries to decipher what the first group is trying to say.

The groups switch roles from time to time so that everyone gets the chance to be histrionic and contorted. Body English encourages discussion, decision making, and cooperation.

4-Way Tug of War Ropes (or The Unholy Alliance)***

Use of these special 1" diameter ropes often precludes the pull-off-your-arms contests so characteristic of a single rope tug-of-war. With 4 teams of up to 15 participants each, players are able to develop strategies and temporary affiliations that bring people back for "just one more try."

How to Use the Alliance Tug Rope

Cut a 100' length of ¼" polypropalene (or some such cord) and tie the ends together (splicing looks better) to form a rope circle as it lies on the ground. Marking every 25' of this rope length, with tape, change the circle to a square. This rope square designates the boundary marker. Use tent stakes at the taped corners to form and hold the square.

Since each of the 4 pulling ropes is only 30' long, it doesn't make much sense to put more than 15 pullers on a length—there just isn't room for more to pull efficiently. Split the group into 4 equal smaller groups and ask them to assume the pull position (whatever that means). Do not allow the last person to tie into the rope. As a matter of further safety, don't allow any knots to be tied in any of the ropes.

As the Pull Master (PM), take the 4 pulling ropes and set the center ring (the drop forged steel ring to which all four ropes are spliced) in the center of the boundary square so that the 4 ropes bisect and are perpendicular to the 4 sides of the boundary square. Refer to photo:

The PM advises, "take up the strain," at which time all pullers slowly begin to put pressure on the ropes. After a couple seconds of holding the rings on center and as the pressure increases, the PM shouts PULL and quickly steps back.

The deception and strategy during the first pull-off usually gives way to pure energy as the teams exhaust themselves (and one another) by pulling against each other at right angles. It takes a couple of pull-offs for a group to discover how brief alliances with the pulling teams to their right and left can produce victory for their team. This very physical contest is an announced anti-trust activity.

A win is achieved when a team pulls the center ring over the section of boundary rope that marks their part of the square. If the rings go directly over any of the 4 right angles, it is a NO PULL, and the teams begin again from a starting position.

Make sure you let the teams try this activity often enough so that team strategies can develop.

Suggest game variations such as mano-a-mano; i.e., pitting 4 people against one another with one puller on each rope. Establish tag teams of different sizes or opposite sex or mixed doubles; experiment.

If you are the Pull Master, watch out when you yell PULL at the start, as rapid movement of the ring can result in a horizontal PM.

If you plan to put together your own 4-way pull ropes, please be sure to choose rope that is advertised as stronger than the estimated combined pulling power of the participants. I also suggest using metal thimbles for the splices and a $5/8''$ drop forged metal diameter ring in the center.

This activity is physically exhausting—don't count on over 30 minutes of participation.

Shoot Out**

This game can have either a lot of rules or very few, depending upon how it's presented and "where the players are at."

If the group is into fantasy and fun, the extra rules and ritual are usually well received. If the group is young and active, they will want action and less explanation.

Give the groups what they want—it's a good workout either way.

General Rules (add or subtract appropriately).

The playing area can be inside a gym (field house) or on a marked field (football, etc.). There seems to be a certain intimacy (trapped feeling) gained from playing inside a gym.

You need two teams of about 5-15 people. The old "skins and shirts" team split works well for this game; i.e., male versus female.

Separate the two teams (however you decide to divide the group) and give each member a frisbee (plastic flying saucer), making sure that each member of a team has the same color saucer.

At this juncture, explain to the team that they must come up with a verbal insult to hurl at the other group. The insult may include no obscene words or ethnic slurs and is delivered in unison or by the chosen DI (designated insulter).

After some in-depth insult discussion, the opposing groups line up facing each other about 30 yards apart. All *Shoot Out* participants must, at this point, holster their frisbees. This is done by sticking the saucer into the waist belt of their shorts, pants, etc., in such a way that a quick draw can be accomplished. (Gentlemen should be aware that shoving the frisbee too far down into their "holster" might result in a pre-game injury that could remove them from the competition. Substitutions are not allowed, so be careful).

As both groups ritualistically glare at one another, the signal to begin is given. All members, of opposite groups, slowly stalk toward one another (VERY purposefully—you

know, like in *High Noon, Gunfight at the OK Corral*, etc.,), until they reach a line that separates the groups by about 10 yards. When both groups are aligned, the DI says, "When you were a baby, you were sooo ugly your mother fed you with a slingshot!" or some-such invective. The responding group, shocked and infuriated by such an incisive remark, says in unison, "Oh, yeah?!" This traditional and expected response is the signal for everyone to go for his/her frisbee, which weapon *must* be thrown within 2 seconds after the first frisbee is released, and certainly before a step is taken.

If a thrown saucer hits a player below the waist, he/she must die a dramatic, histrionic and noisy death (like in *Rio Lobo, The Magnificent Seven,* or more recently *A Fist Full of Dollars*), and lie on the floor or field until that segment of the game is concluded.

After a red or blue saucer is released, only that color may be picked up by a team member as the participants dash about trying to find a thrown weapon and, at the same time, protect themselves. Players may knock a thrown saucer aside with a saucer, but may not catch a frisbee that has been thrown at them.

Play continues until all members of one group have been properly "drilled,"

"plugged"; i.e., eliminated. If the players seem interested, a win or lose announcement can be made, but the results are self-evident and only momentarily significant. The groups then realign themselves at opposite ends of the field to discuss strategy and prepare to give or receive the next insult.

There is obviously a lot of tradition and ritual that must be enjoyed (relived) to make the game "work." If the group is young and more into activity than tradition—line them up as before (10 yards) and let them blast away at a given signal.

This game can also be played "one-on-one." In such a confrontation, the two players make their own rules. For example: each player carries 2 saucers; a hit must be below the knee; start as in a duel; i.e., back-to-back, etc. Use flexible saucers, marshmallows, or nerf balls in place of frisbees if there seems to be a danger of hard, uncontrolled throws.

Rule #1 - Use a large Nerf ball as the throwing object.
Rule #2 - Head shots don't count.
Now, let's play!

Someone starts by being IT. IT tries to eliminate players by hitting them with the ball. If hit, a person must sit down on the floor "indian style." The afflicted person remains in this legs-crossed position unless they can snag a thrown ball, at which point they are armed and back in the game.

IT cannot run with the ball; only pivot and throw. Being a basically good sport, IT cannot (would not) deliberately roll a ball to a seated person. A variation allows moving by dribbling the ball. Have your ever tried dribbling a Nerf ball?

Include two or more balls for increased action.

Full House*

This mini-bombardment game has been played during a number of adventure workshops with enthusiastic results. A large house or gymnasium is best suited for the fast-paced action, but a heavily wooded area also has appeal. In a pinch, I suspect an open field would be suitable, too.

You need a few articles of play—weapons, actually. For this soft war action, tinted (two color) marshmallows offer a safe and tasty throwing implement for freezing (cryogenic suspension) your opponent.

Two equally numbered teams separate and go to opposite ends of a house, gym, field, etc. Each team member is given 3 marshmallows of a particular color (red team — blue team) and instructed to try and get to the opposite side of the house, gym, field; a designated SAFE area. The first team to move all its players into the SAFE area gets

to eat their weapons and/or receive eatable team trophies. Two-week-old weapons are a questionable taste treat—flambé is the gourmet's solution.

As the players are passing (sneaking) by each other, they can freeze opposing team members by hitting them with a thrown marshmallow (anywhere below the neck). A cyrogenically suspended player must remain immobile for 30 seconds after being hit. Players may only collect and throw marshmallows of their team's color.

You can probably imagine the potential for fun as players run upstairs, through open doorways and zip down halls, hotly pursuing one another with their gaily tinted *objects du guerre*.

Use blindfolds as headbands to differentiate team members. Remember, that's blindfolds as headbands, not vice-versa.

Boffer Bonkers***

This simplistic, blatantly competitive game is one of the most aerobic and least serious one-on-one confrontations I've played. Bonkers can be played as teams, but the pure form is one balloon, two players. Action on a gym floor is most convenient because of the permanent boundary lines. Use the center line of a basketball court to place your well-inflated balloons (a 12″ balloon works best—penny balloons don't provide enough action). Both players, armed with a foam sword, back off to the next parallel line—I'm sure this line has a name, but you'll recognize it because it looks very much like the one that you put the balloon on. The playing area is designated by the distance from one back line to another.

Play begins as each of the two players, standing on his/her back line, and facing the other player, ritualistically slams his/her boffer against the floor three times in rhythm with the other player's similar efforts. On the third hit, both players rush forward and try to hit the balloon past their opponents' back line *so that the balloon hits the floor* beyond that line. A player on offense is not allowed to physically cross over his/her opponent's back line.

A point is scored when the balloon touches the floor beyond the back line. Best two out of three points is guaranteed to bring your heart rate up to 160 BPM.

Aggression Bonkers allows a player to cross over his/her opponent's back line. A point is then scored either by hitting the balloon to the floor (as before) or bouncing the balloon off the back wall. If you are playing on an outdoor basketball court, the back wall rule is waived—a winning shot in this case puts the balloon off the court; i.e., out of bounds.

If you wish to play Team Bonkers, simply supply more people with foam swords. (Do not substitute 2 x 4's for regulation Boffers, because splinters may cause the balloons to burst.)

The balloons do break occasionally, so be sure to have inflated ones in reserve to keep the game moving.

Tusker or Add-On-Tag**

The object of this running game for 10-30 players is for one IT pair of hand-in-hand runners to catch a fleeing pair and become a catching quartet (hands joined to form a line) and then catch another pair to become a sextet, etc. Only the two people at the end of the catching line are allowed to tag a fleeing pair, (one hand anywhere . . . well, almost anywhere). If the line breaks at any point, a catch is disallowed. This catching sequence continues until only one pair is left and, as undisputed champions of speed and chicanery, become exempt from further chase and harassment.

If a running pair breaks grip or runs out of bounds, they are automatically caught. To prevent injury, do not allow pairs to run through or under the catching line. Restrict the playing area so that the game is active, but not so small that the catching line becomes an encompassing seine. In the past, I have set up three fixed boundary lines and left the fourth boundary to be an imaginary line marked by my extended arm presence. This allows a comparatively small play area to begin with (when it's hard for a single pair to catch another pair) and an incrementally growing area, as I occasionally and unobtrusively shuffle a few feet back. The students are so involved with the game that no one notices a gradual extension of the boundaries. (I haven't been caught yet!)

Add-on Tag Variations:

(a) Offer a foam sword (tusk) to the catchers at each end of the line. This extends their reach and adds a bit of consequence to being caught (whacked). Experiencing a double-tusked catching line cornering you and your equally-panicked partner is an adrenalin-pumper—a few benign squirts of adrenalin beats a caffeine high any day.

(b) Tell the developing line of frothing catchers that they are allowed to pivot; i.e. everyone breaking grips, doing an about-face, regripping, and "tally ho."

(c) Allow the catching line to break apart after a predetermined number of people join the line. For example, when 8 players are joined, they split in half, forming two catching groups of 4. This halving at 8 continues until the game is over. This variation is called *BLOB* by the New Games folks. After this game has been played a few times, it becomes obvious to most that the greatest problem involved in catching the fleeing pairs is not speed or strength but communication and group coordination. It's worth talking about with the group.

42

44

Samurai & a Kamikaze Variation***

The game, Samurai, is explained and pictured in the *More New Games* book, made available by the New Games Foundation of California. Samurai has become a workshop favorite of mine. In addition, a recent Project Adventure workshop group developed an embellishment to the game that is worth passing along.

There are a number of game success ingredients included in Samurai that almost guarantee acceptance and active participation by almost any group.

1. Rules can be quickly explained and easily understood.
2. Participants can unobtrusively remove themselves from the game.
3. Role-playing is encouraged and applauded.
4. Simple physical skills are used.
5. Satisfaction results from participation or observing.

A bare-bones description of the basic game follows (refer to the *More New Games* book for additional details):

Ask your group to form a circle around you—about 4' - 6' between people. Armed with a boffer (ideally) or any easily manipulated and innocuous sword-like weapon, the person in the center attempts to eliminate everyone in the circle with high or low slashes of their ersatz sword. These slashes are token strokes only; actual contact must be avoided or the players in the circle will either lose trust and disperse, or lose trust and retaliate.

If the Samurai (person with the sword) slashes high, each participant included within the arc of the stroke must duck or lose his/her head and be eliminated (falling to the ground). If the sweep of the sword is low, a hop must be made or the legs are removed, as is the player. All of this martial manipulation is accompanied by the inscrutable yells of the Samurai and groans of dismay and simulated agony of the players—a cacophony of oral action and reaction.

This last person to remain standing is the next Samurai.

After the basic game has been played a couple of times, try this kamikaze variation called *Samurai Suicide.*

As the game begins, place a second sword on the ground in the center of the circle. As the Samurai begins his/her circular sanguinary forays, anyone in the circle can try to grab the second sword (boffer) without being hit (actually hit) by the Samurai's sword. Then, mouthing whatever challenge or simulated invective comes to mind, the two adversaries have at one another in a duel to the finish.

Rules for the Duel:
1. No slashing strokes allowed—only thrusts to the torso.
2. A win is achieved by touching your opponent, with the tip of the boffer, on the torso only—head and appendages do not count as a touché.
3. Do not use a rigid pretend sword for this duel.

If the Samurai wins, the opponent joins the other vanquished players and places his/her sword back in the center.

If the sword-snatcher wins, all the previously truncated players return to the game, and the new Samurai must begin again against a full circle of players.

Texas Big Foot*

Need a simplistic task that can't be done (almost can't be done)? Texas Big Foot takes little time to explain or attempt and provides a humorous low-key task that is apt to fail. If personal expectations aren't paramount and image is not on self-destruct, it's sometimes fun to fail—particularly as a group.

Ask the group to form a circle (with you included) so that everyone is holding onto partners on both sides—arms around shoulders. Then announce that this activity is extremely difficult to accomplish and that morphological co-operation is essential to success and avoidance of injury. Indicate that to accomplish the task the group has to (in their present arm-over-shoulder configuration) take three giant steps toward the center of the circle. To be successful, the final step must end with the group still intact and standing.

Count off the first step, then stop. Give encouragement and praise. Count the second step—no comments are necessary or useful at this point because of the laughter and convolution of the former circle. The final giant step invariably results in falling down by some participants or complete disfiguration of the circle; i.e., failure to achieve the announced goal.

Admittedly a "lightweight" activity, but a nice tone-setter toward sharing laughter and unselfconscious touching.

46

Tickle-a-Pickle*

This quick laughter-producer is a natural follow-up to Texas Big Foot.

As the group collapses at the end of the third step, ask them to pack closely together (cluster) and pretend briefly that they are pickles in a small jar. There is only one thing to do in that type of situation—the instructor initiates a quick tickle move on someone saying loudly, "Tickle-a-pickle." Tickling attempts sweep through the group as finger forays and guffawed escapes run rampant.

Shark*

There are innumerable games to try using a cordless parachute, and many of them are so simplistic as to be a bit tedious, but this one plucked my sense of humor and macabre fantasy. It is of the touch me/don't touch me or humor/horror genre.

As a group, stand in a circle, holding the edges of the parachute (is there any other way?) and sit down on the gym floor, pulling the edges of the chute up to your waist with your legs underneath.

Ask a person to act as the SHARK. This nefarious individual scoots under the chute and begins patrolling the confines of the chute's perimeter (the SHARK pool). When the shark spies a pair of feet that look delectable, she/he *grabs* those appendages and while alternately squeezing and relaxing their grip (chewing motion), the SHARK pulls the victim under the chute to join as a zombie shark. All this is accomplished amidst much screaming and thrashing about by the victim. Then, these *two* sharks continue patrolling the pool, looking for more wiggling meat. Continue play until the last victim becomes the next shark.

Seeing a "shark" slowly approach your feet produces a surprisingly tense feeling. Being grabbed, finally, gives you a chance to release your anxiety by acting like a victim.

Indicate to your sharks that subtly cruising the pool adds considerably to the activity; i.e., don't grab every leg you pass by.

Tug-O-War*

A parachute quickie that doesn't work if your chute has holes in it—the holes get bigger, fast . . . .

If your chute is divided into colors, setting up the contest is easy. Reds against whites, or reds against yellows against whites, etc.

Whatever—simply have your group securely grasp the edge of the chute and pull with their "team" until one group pulls another group steadily in one direction. Watching the amount of tension applied to the rip-stop nylon and the stitches gives an idea of how well made a parachute must be.

Cat and Mouse*

47

Position: Group kneels around the perimeter of a parachute and grasps the edge.

Object: For a mouse to stay hidden (uncaught) under the parachute while a cat, crawling on top of the parachute, tries to pounce on the mouse. The group tries to help the mouse by rapidly shaking the folds of the parachute up and down. Such irregular wave-like motion gives the mouse some hiding space and is confusing for the cat.

Where-Am-I?*

Position: As in Cat and Mouse, except standing.

Object: For a blindfolded person, standing on top of and in the center of the parachute, to try and find the only path out of the parachute. The path is designated by one or two people holding their piece of the parachute's arc to the floor, while the other standing folks moderately flap their sections up and down.

Verbal sound effects of a violent storm add to the realism and make the task more challenging and fun. If your gym floor is dusty or dirty, for the sake of everyone's respiratory health, skip the last two activities or clean the place up a bit.

Balloons are fun and they are cheap (compared to Earth Balls). Get a gross and try these games. (Quality balloons are considerably less expensive when purchased by the gross.)

Booop***

Blow up *one* of the balloons and tie off the neck. Ask your group of 4-6 people to join hands in a circle and try to keep the balloon aloft (off the floor) by batting the balloon with any parts of their body, including hands which must remain clasped. If the balloon touches the floor, the group loses use of their hands. As balloons continue to eventually and inevitably fall to the floor, keep removing parts of the anatomy that are allowed to strike the balloon; for example, elbows, shoulders, head, thigh, etc. The group that eventually loses use of their feet is out and can then recycle to any point of the game they choose. Watch for high kicks in a small circle.

Addition to *BOOOP*

For you trivia buffs, the name BOOOP comes from the sound of an elbow hitting a balloon.

Another variation requires the group to sit on the floor while boooping the balloons. As a last means of keeping the balloons aloft, allow no body contact, only air pressure; i.e., blowing. Another approach allows a designated person to call out BOOOP Commands. For example: Hands only; heads only (then clockwise & counter clockwise); sit down and toes only; on your back and hands only, etc. Continue, using as many parts of the anatomy as possible. This is a functional variation in that misses or mistakes have no consequence except laughter.

Finish by ordering the groups to see how long they can keep a balloon off the floor by blowing only.

49

BRAAAAAAACK- WHFFFFF*

Everyone gets one balloon. The balloon should be purchased in as many different colors as possible; ecru, vermillion, puce, etc. Also, buy decent sized balloons; small ones don't remain aloft very long or provide enough action for these games.

The Game

Ask everyone to stand inside the "key" at the end of a basketball court (or fabricate your own round boundary area), and blow up their balloons just short of popping. (Have some spare balloons available.) Don't tie off the balloon's neck, just hold on and get together with other folks who have the same color balloon as yours.

One player, representing one team's color (you can have as many teams as you have colored balloons) and standing within the circle area, lets go of his/her balloon, allowing it to jet willy-nilly about. As the limp projectile comes to rest, another team member of the same color advances to that point with filled balloon and releases the rubber missile in an attempt to further their team's distance from the circle's perimeter. Try launching your balloon like a football: it doesn't add any distance, but it makes you feel like you are doing something.

This sequence continues until all the balloons have been released. The team color champion is, of course, that final balloon which is the furthest from the circle. (Have a 50' tape measure on hand for disputed distances.)

There is practically no skill involved in this game, so no one seems to care who wins. The fun is in the doing.

PLYNN

50

Fire in the Hole***

It's time to put the balloons away—permanently. You're going to like this! Divide into groups of 3-5.

Place 3-5 balloons between your 3-5 person group. Position the balloons carefully at about midtorso level. As in dealing with dynamite charges, it's the placement that counts. Then, put your arms about your partners' bodies and prepare to squeeze, BUT . . . before initiating any gross psycho-motor movement, the group shouts together, "Fire in the hole"—that's to warn any bystanders of the impending explosion(s). You don't need any further instructions after the squeeze starts.

If a particular balloon is giving your small group a problem, ask for help from other squeezers. I'm sure, volunteers will hurry over to add their contractions and emotions toward a final solution. One-on-one Fire-in-the-Hole is an intense experience to be savored with a special partner.

Fire-in-the-Hole can be used successfully in a number of hilarious and meaningless ways, including: on a dance floor; on rappel; in a pool and en masse on a wrestling mat. Truly a game for all seasons, and not many reasons.

Object: For an unknown killer to "kill" all the people involved in the game, before they discover who she/he is.

Set-up: There are many ways to pick a killer, but the easiest and fastest is for the leader to ask all the players to close their eyes, and then walk briskly and obviously around and among the players, touching one of them on top of the head to indicate his/her sanguine role.

Rules:

To kill, the killer must wink at a player. If the wink (not a blink) is recognized as the gift of eternal sleep, that player is dead and must histrionically die, ending up flailing about or shuddering on the floor/ground while emitting outrageous sounds of agony, outrage and defeat: this is not meant to be a subtle role. DO NOT die immediately after being killed. Give the killer a chance to move away by waiting 15-30 seconds until your terminal sequence begins.

As the group mills about the playing area, eyeing each other carefully (you must keep your eyes open), and someone thinks he/she knows who the killer is, he/she shouts, "I accuse!" The accuser must be seconded by another player within ten seconds or the initial accuser is eliminated (bumped off) by the referee's (your) pearl-handled revolver.

However, if there is a second, you (the referee) say, "On the count of three, I want you both to point accusingly at the killer." If both players point at the same person and it is, indeed, the mass murderer—the game is over. If the accusers point at different people, you quickly reach for your revolver and polish off the two maladroits who have so crassly offended the group's sensibilities. The game continues until the killer is caught or until all the players have been killed; a feat worthy of applause and a couple of rousing "good shows."

Variations:

1. Allow the killer to pass on the death knell by shaking hands and pressing the victim's wrist with an extended index finger. It is obviously not necessary to kill every time a hand is shaken.

So then, here we go about the room en-thusiastically shaking hands with everyone and looking frantically for the deadly digit. All the above rules for basic killer apply here.

2. If the vibrations of all this noise and cascading bodies is distressing, try this "nice" variation.

Everyone in the group must go around the room whispering something nice to each player encountered. The exception, of course, is the killer, who will whisper something pejorative having to do with one's demise. For example, "I sure like your knees," or "That blouse is outstanding," or "Your crew cut is cute." The killer might say, "Here comes the kiss of death," or "Tomorrow you die," etc.

3. If the games are dragging a bit and you want to speed things up, introduce the plague variation.

Whenever a player is killed, she/he can (after waiting a few seconds to let the killer move on), take another player down as she/he falls to the floor by touching someone (the plague). That infected player can then pass it on to another poor soul if she/he is slow enough to be caught. The dying person cannot run around the room tagging a series of people, nor can the initial person with the plague fall on the killer. If the killer carelessly gets caught in a plague sequence, then it's either fast-talking time or just keeping a low profile.

4. If your group is going to be together for over 24 hours (camp, seminar, workshop), try "24 hour Killer." In this variation of the game, which lasts a full 1,440 minutes, there are two new means of ersatz homicide.

a. Since some friendly folk are turned off by the violence of killing, there is another means of participant termination called the "Kiss of Death." The killer, in this case, simply delivers a full-lipped smooch (as if throwing a kiss, but with exaggerated lip movements) to the victim. The affectionately terminated player has the remainder of the game to choose an appropriate death scene. Some of the macabre sequences that have been attempted over the years are unbelievable in scope and imagination. (I'll not attempt to revive them in writing, as I'm sure you will see them all if you play the game often enough.) The lip-kiss-kill is difficult to conceal, so the killer must be subtle and sneaky.

b. The second killing sign is accomplished by making the OK sign with your index finger and thumb, and placing that digital symbol (your hand) anywhere on *your* body below the waist. The "kill" is accomplished if a player makes eye contact with your hand. Group killing possibilities are endless.

From previous experiences, I'd suggest excluding death sequences from eating areas and also ask the players not to make their demise so realistic as to initiate first aid attempts; i.e., choking, apoplexy, convulsions, etc.

At the end of 24 hours, it's worth asking the group to relate humorous or inventive ploys used by the killer—and, also to ask each killer what he/she thought of the role and its ramifications within the group and structure of the workshop.

It may seem that everyone gets in on the fun of these games except you—so here's a way to pick the killer and join in the game yourself.

Everyone joins together in a cluster and puts one fist into the center with a thumb sticking up. You announce (with everyone's eyes closed, including yours) that you are going to squeeze a person's thumb once. That person then will reach around all the extended thumbs (all eyes still closed) and squeeze someone else's thumb twice. The person with the double-squeezed digit is the killer. Neat, huh?

Play *Killer* more than once to discover some of the subtleties and strategems that make this game so popular.

Hands Down***

People generally see what they want to see or only what is being shown to them. From the standpoint of trying to solve an initiative problem, such tunnel vision results in frustration and limited success.

This simple problem (demonstration, actually) is designed to point out that immediately observable facts are not necessarily the combination needed for a solution.

Obtain five lengths (about 6") of any type of matching material (e.g., pencils, dowels, sticks). Kneel down on the floor, pavement, ground, and place the five pencils on the flat area in front of you so that a pattern is formed—any pattern will do. For example:

or whatever your imagination produces. Ask the group surrounding you to indicate the number from one to ten that this arrangement of sticks demonstrates. Set up two or three different patterns so that the group gets to see and guess additional numbers that you are depicting.

The gimmick—Set down whatever fanciful combination or pattern of sticks your imagination conjures up, placing your hands, palms down, on the floor next to the sticks with the number of fingers exposed indicating the number you have in mind. The sticks do not indicate anything. Change the pattern of sticks and change the number of fingers you extend (two fists on the ground is zero; two hands down with all fingers extended is ten).

Someone will eventually figure out what you are doing. Use that person to maintain group interest by asking him/her to name the number indicated by each new pattern. If no one catches on after a few patterns, place your hands closer to the sticks or eventually throw the sticks on the floor and ostentatiously slap your palms on the area in front of you. People standing behind you are generally the first to figure out the gimmick.

Be sure to finish up this exercise with a brief statement of what you were trying to accomplish, and what the gimmick was, because inevitably there will be a couple of folks still baffled by your covert "digital" display.

Bang, You're Dead*

This game and many like it belong to the I-know-there's-a-clue-but-I-can't-figure-it-out collection.

The object is for a group to figure out why whatever you're saying is true or why their reply is wrong.

In this particular game, for example, you say, "Bang, You're Dead!" and then wait for a response from someone in the group indicating whom they think you shot. The guesses begin slowly and the frustration level grows apace as you indicate through yes-no answers, apparently without reason, who has been shot. Then you begin again with another "Bang, You're Dead!" exclamation, pointing gun finger and headfake.

The clue in this particular game is, whoever makes the first verbal response to your "Bang . . . ." is the victim. Too easy? Try the game and see how long it takes for the group to figure it out. Remember, "Truth is obvious, after its discovery."

Other clues in additional games of this type could be body or limb positions. If the group becomes adept at spotting clues, try using "eraser clues"; i.e., body movements or positions that indicate just the opposite for a clue. Example: If your legs are crossed, then an uncrossed leg position is the key. And then try double eraser clues . . . .

Passing Crossed or Uncrossed*

This around-the-campfire game is historically played with a pair of scissors, but can be as effectively played with two pencils, two sticks, etc.

A leader initiates the activity by passing two pencils to the person sitting to their left or right in the circle. The leader says one of two things, "I am passing these pencils to you crossed," or "I am passing these pencils to you uncrossed." The leader indicates to the group that each person is to individually receive the pencils and then pass them on crossed or uncrossed, also verbally stating both how they were received and how they are being passed; i.e., crossed or uncrossed.

Confusion begins when a player receives the pencils parallel to one another and the passer says, "I am passing these pencils to you crossed." The group looks to you for confirmation that this person is bewildered. Your confirmation of the passer's correct assessment and action increases the confusion. Why are obviously uncrossed pencils being passed "crossed"? As in all these where-is-the-key problems, the obvious pencils have nothing to do with the crossed or uncrossed situation.

The "key" is the leg position of the person doing the passing and the leg position of that person to whom they are being passed. For example, the person receiving the pencils says, "I am receiving these pencils crossed." (Are the passer's legs *crossed* or uncrossed?) and "I am passing them on uncrossed." (Are the receiver's legs crossed or uncrossed?)

"'I see,' said the blind man, as he picked up his hammer and saw."

I've Got the Beat**

Utilizing any object or even your own finger, establish a simple beat by striking that object on a table, floor, etc. There should be no more than 8-12 movements to the beat. Perform the movements of the beat a couple times in front of your group so that they have a chance to understand what you are doing. After you have performed the sequence a few times tell them that, "I've got the beat." Then offer them the object to tap with and ask if anyone else thinks they have the beat. If your beat sequence is simple enough you will have a couple volunteers who think they can duplicate your actions.

As in all these do-as-I-do problems the key is not the obvious movement, but is revealed as a pre or post movement or sound. In this case a *deep breath* before starting the beat is the indication or key to a "successful" beat. The key can be any number of things, but the group must begin to realize that the answer to these types of problems (and many initiative type problems) is often not the visually obvious one.

Predictably the people who think they know how to duplicate your beat are concentrating on exactly what your physical motions are with the beat objects. If, after a few tries, no one has "the beat," make the *deep breath* before starting more obvious. It is amazing how zeroed in some people can become to extraneous actions that they think are the essential movements. As obvious as you think your actions are in trying to expose the "key," there will still be some myopic individuals that say, "Do it one more time." I can commiserate, having been that short-sighted person more often than I'd like to admit.

Nerf Ball Knockaround*

This game works as well on a field as in a gym. The use of a nerf soccer ball allows those youngsters who are afraid of the speed and momentum of a regulation ball to participate without worrying about getting bopped on the nose. The rules are simple, and hooray for that.

Set out two street hockey nets a distance apart that makes sense for your available area. Divide your group into two teams without employing the sociogram technique of choosing up sides. Then differentiate the teams with pinneys, rolled up pants, hat/no hats, blue pants/other color pants—not male/female, please! Throw out two nerf soccer balls and play regular soccer rules. When a goal is scored, you record the goal and throw the ball back in play near the center of the field. In this way, there is no need to stop the action. If you are part of the action, so much the better.

Tegwar

Tegwar is an acronym for, That-Exiting-Game-Without-Any-Rules, and as a game it presents a classic mental/physical exercise in logical confusion. Any obvious lack of rules within or surrounding a game requires a fairly complex set of non-rules or acceptable confusers to make play possible.

For example, if you are going to plan a Tegwar variation of soccer, (and you can't really, because Tegwar is Tegwar and only alludes to soccer in order to explain Tegwar) you must ignore all the rules, better yet recognize that there are no rules, and then establish touchstones of play; i.e., those gems of illogic points of concentration. To score or make a good play is an illusion that lasts only long enough to feel good and then melds into the next acceptable sequence of physical action. Recognizing that there are no established guidelines and operating meaningfully within a game context without consistent regulations is the key to understanding how an unorganized semi-serious potpourri of play can be exciting and fun without any rules.

I've burdened you with all this twaddle to simply indicate that Tegwar is child's play, which is probably the best kind. Think of the above as a round-about introduction to an initiative problem. Take any game and reduce or change the rules to that point where the structure of the game remains intact, *all* participants feel good about being part of the action, and the joy remains or has increased. A formidable task, but it's worth a try or two, and who knows what might emerge. It's better than running laps.

Trash Ball*

Another esoteric game for the Mensa group.

Divide your group in half and situate them on opposite sides of a volleyball net. (Fortunately, the playing dimensions of a volleyball court exactly duplicate the NCAA Trash Ball specs.) Offer each group an equal amount of *dry* trash. (There is a wet trash variation of this game called *Garbage Ball*, but permission slips from parents and custodians are required.) An example of dry trash is—wastepaper, cardboard boxes, light plastic, etc.

Make sure there is an ample amount of trash: trash equals action.

On the GO signal, each team tries to put their trash over the net. Do not set a time limit for the game, rather indicate that you will signal when the game is over. This unexpected signal prevents a team from collecting all the trash and throwing it over the net seconds before the time limit.

The winner is, justly, that team with the least amount of trash within bounds on their side of the net. So that the teams won't suspect favoritism by the referee, the ref must write down on a sheet of paper the proposed time limit for each game.

This melee of low key physical misdirection and laughter is a philosophical breakthrough in experiential education, ranking right up there with Mud Wrestling.

Hula Hoops or More Hoops than Hula

It appears that not many folks use "Hula Hoops" for hip spinning now-a-days, although keeping that infernal circle above my hips is still a task that befuddles my lower anatomy. Curious storekeepers now ask, "What are you going to use them for?" as scientists, educators, mathematicians and recreation specialists find an increasing number of uses for these simple but intriguing plastic hoops.

Rodeo Throw**

Try the following activity on a wooden gym floor (a rubberized gym floor provides too much friction). Throw a hoop away from you with an underhand motion and in the same motion impart a backward spin to the hoop. The hoop will travel—rapidly spinning and gently bouncing—away from the thrower until the backward spinning motion overcomes forward momentum, causing the hoop to spin in place for a couple seconds and eventually return in the general direction of the thrower.

Practicing this type of throw is preliminary training for the next event: the *Rodeo Throw*. Try to have lots of hoops on hand to include as many people as possible.

Two participants stand next to one another at one end of a gym; one as the runner and the other as thrower. The thrower spins the hoop on the floor (as above) and the runner attempts to sprint out and dive through the vertically spinning hoop without knocking it over. Timing is important, as the best chance to scamper through the hoop is when it briefly spins in place. Two trips through the hoop is possible but requires a good throw, quick feet, and/or a small bod.

Variations quickly present themselves from this simple beginning as people align themselves differently (opposite ends of the gym for simultaneous throws and dives) or try increasingly difficult tricks (feet first through the spinning hoop).

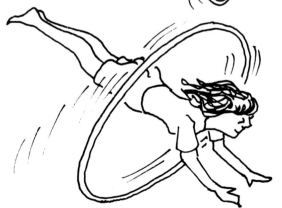

PLYNN

Circle the Circle**

Ask the group (15-30) to form a hand-in-hand circle. Place two large hoops together between two people (resting on their grasped hands). See how quickly the participants in the circle can cause the hoops to travel around the circle (over the people) in opposite directions, through each other (i.e., hoop through hoop) and back to the originating point. Use fairly large hoops for this activity—they are sold in different diameters.

It's interesting to see what the group's response is when you ask, "Who won?" after both hoops have circled the circle. It takes some thought to realize that the entire group is working as a team. No losers. No winners.

Hoop Relay*

Divide the group into two parts and ask each half to queue up facing you. The folks in each file should be holding hands front-to-back; i.e., reaching backward through their legs to grasp the free hand of the person behind them. This relay requires two starters, each standing in front of a line, designating the start, and each holding 3-4 hoops. Each starter, on a signal, begins the action by placing a hoop over the head of the first person in line and as soon as that hoop has been moved to the third person in line, the second hoop is started, etc. If the starters want to become part of the action they simply start the last hoop and become the first person in line. When the first hoop reaches the last person in line, that individual runs to the front of the line with the hoop, grabs the hand of the now second person and starts the hoop moving toward the end of the line. Continue until the original front line person returns to that position.

PLYNN

Quail Shooter's Delight***

If you know you are going to fail, it makes trying less of a trauma.

The object of this throw and catch game is to grab as many of the thrown objects as possible and hold onto them. The not-so-obvious rationale is to provide a low-key vehicle for unselfconscious participation.

Ask 2 or 3 people to stand back-to-back in the center of a people circle that measures about 30' in diameter. The number of people in the middle and the circle size will vary according to the numbers playing.

Using easily throwable and comparatively innocuous objects (frisbees, foldable saucers, nerf balls, knotted towels, etc.), ask each person on the circle's periphery to pick up one or two of the "balls." On the count of 3, the group *simultaneously* lofts the throwing object toward the 2-3 waiting targets. The catchers attempt to see how many of the flying objects they can hold onto. The results are predictably bad, and some worse than others, but everyone expects it (after the first few tries) and the sequential ineptness adds to the fun. The people who haven't tried think they *must* be able to do better than their predecessors. Techniques and attempts abound with pretty much the same result—much grasping, no grabbing.

Set daily world records. With 30 people throwing and two catching, I have yet to see 8 objects caught. It's not uncommon for all 3 catchers to end up empty-handed.

63

Catch 10**

Here's a fast-paced, blatantly competitive game for 3-6 people, that I remember developing with a group of friends on the beaches of southern California many years ago. At that time, we used a football and that's still a good idea, but with a diverse group you may have more luck using a frisbee (the 97 gm model, of course).

The playing area can be any field area that doesn't have a lot of obstacles to run into or trip over. There are no boundaries. Grass, as in most active outdoor games, is the best playing surface, unless a beach is handy (and that is absolutely the ultimate barefoot surface for jump-around, feel good, land-on-your-head games).

The object is to try and make the person you are throwing to miss the frisbee; for which slip of the fingers a point is disawarded. When a player accrues 10 points, she/he is out and the remainder of the players continue until only one remains: numero uno, el campion del mundo.

The throws are made in keeping with a pre-game determined sequence (Pete to Jill, to Rod, to Liz) and continues this way unless a player who has just missed a frisbee thinks he/she has been taken advantage of for one reason or another and shouts "Challenge." The offended player gets to make a standing throw with the frisbee at the person who made him/her miss, from a measured distance of 10 yards. In the event of either a miss or catch, the frisbee continues in the new throw/catch sequence direction; i.e., opposite to the way it was going.

Gentlemen's rules are in effect throughout; i.e., when a throw is made, the catcher must exert a 100% effort to snare the frisbee, but if the disc still drifts beyond his fingers, the point is added to the thrower's total, and if the catcher obviously "dogs it" or short-arms an attempt, the disaward is his.

Catch 10 strategy—Running toward the person you are throwing to is okay and is actually a good offensive move, but a pursuing player must throw the frisbee from a distance of at least 10 yards away from the catcher. Trying to keep the sun at your back is another bit of gamesmanship that works. Try to make it as much a running/catching game as possible by lofting high throws well beyond where the catcher waits or by running to place yourself, as a potential catcher, near to the person you will be throwing to. Think up strategies, add rules, change rules, breathe hard, sweat!

PLYNN

64

Scooter Swing**

I have observed other people trying this swinging idea in past workshops, but I recently tried it myself and can now attest to what I was observing—people having fun and being challenged.

For this activity, you will need a floor scooter (essentially a 12″ x 12″ section of ¾″ plywood that has four ball-bearing casters attached on the bottom of the plywood in each corner) and a dangling rope somewhere near the center of the gym. Use of the 20′ gymnastic climbing ropes will work fine. You will also need a person wearing a helmet, and lots of other folks to stand in a circle around that person. (Brief reference to the helmet situation, because I'm sure it caught your attention. In some instances of adventure programming, you are safer with a helmet on, and this is one of those times. The Scooter Swing activity is not dangerous, but an unplanned fall to the hard floor is possible.)

Ask the group to make a large people-circle around the rope to be used. The chosen participant stands on top of the scooter and grips the rope. Someone walks in from the circle and gives the center person a shove, which scoots the rider toward the far circumference of the circle where he/she is pushed back toward the other side of the circle. This compassionate pushing and scooting continues until the person tires of the ride or falls off the scooter. As long as the rider holds onto the rope, a fall is simply slipping off the scooter and sliding to a stop. Do not allow riders to use black-soled shoes, or the gym floor will suffer and so will your relations with the custodians.

As the rider becomes more adept, the circumference of the circle can be expanded considerably.

This is fun, folks—give it a try. It's a natural for making up games. Two games to try:
1. After each successful push across the circle, expand the circle's circumference by half a step until the rider eventually slips off the scooter.
2. Place a ten pin (or empty tennis ball can) in the center of the circle. The rider starts on the scooter at the edge of the circle somewhere. The group attempts to knock over the ten pin using the rider as the "bowling ball." The rider tries to miss the ten pin by foot movements and body English. Count the number of shoves necessary to knock over the pin. The circle's circumference remains the same throughout each attempt. The larger the circle is, the more chance the rider has of missing the pin.

65

Scooter Slalom**

Use the same type of scooter explained previously in the Scooter Swing. You will need a minimum of two scooters, but having a few more keeps things moving; i.e., less standing and waiting.

This aerobic activity requires that the students work in pairs. They will be "scooting" through a slalom course set up on the gym floor in an attempt to establish a time. Each additional attempt offers a chance to better their record. Emphasize pair self-satisfaction, because time comparisons with other pairs is inevitable.

The rider sits on a scooter and puts his/her feet on top of a second scooter. The second member of the pair stands behind the rider and provides the GO, by pushing. The slalom course, a sample of which is outlined in the illustration, should include a few right angle turns, a couple "hair pins" and a straightaway—be inventive (tough, but realistic).

A couple of people in the group with digital watches can be timers until their turn comes up. As the pair attempts to make their fastest trip through the slalom markers (cones), it becomes obvious that the pair which works together (the rider uses his/her hands as outriggers to aid balance and turning), shows the most improvement. There is an infectious quality to this activity, because each pair is sure they can "do it faster next time."

Rule

1. One pair on the course at a time.
2. For each pylon or cone touched, a second is added to the total time. If a marker is knocked over, add two seconds.
3. If the rider's feet come off the front scooter and touch the floor, the ride may continue. If the rider's posterior hits the floor, the ride is over.
4. Slingshotting the rider is not allowed.
5. Rider and pusher must maintain physical contact throughout the run . . . . Particularly over the finish line.
6. Riders should wear a helmet.
7. Riders should wear gloves to protect their palms during turns.

Try to set up the slalom cones (using the entire gym floor), so that the start and finish is at the same end of the gym.

As this activity uses up a lot of energy, a pair should be encouraged to switch roles as rider and pusher. This suggestion is usually well received by the pusher.

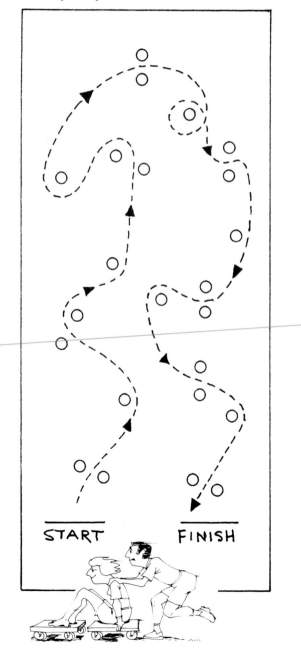

66

Sacky Hack

Undoubtedly one of the most frustrating and infectiously popular and portable pastimes to come from California in a long time is the frenetic, small circle, down-time beater called a Hacky Sack. Essentially the Hacky Sack is a small (about the size of a kiwi fruit) stitched leather-bag filled with cherry pits. I'm not kidding about the pits inside . . . there must be something exotic in there to justify the price tag. Maybe it's the stitching.

The game idea is to kick this small sac or strike it with some part of your body (as in soccer, contact with hands, arms and shoulders is verboten), so that someone else can also experience the personal embarrassment of completely mis-directing this miniscule soccer sac. I will admit that trying to keep the sac aloft for an established number of hits, kicks, etc., is a just-one-more-try affliction that is not only individually insidious but wildly contagious.

You might assume from my irreverant tongue-in-cheek comments about various player's abilities, that use of a Hacky Sack is an elitist activity. Not so! Everyone has the same opportunity to look inept and descended from Son of Maladroit. Skill level obviously increases with practice, but not everyone has 11 hours a day to kick around a pit sack, so here's a suggestion or two for those of you who are employed.

I have invented the Sacky Hack, for us hackers who want almost instant gratification from our physical endeavors. Simply do this. Blow up a balloon that has a couple ounces of water in it and kick away. The sloshing water provides erratic flight characteristics (the challenge), but the size of the balloon allows a better-than-average chance of making contact (the satisfaction). If even this slowed-down version gives you trouble, fill the balloon with helium, and after the first kick it will disappear, providing you with the opportunity to seek other diversions that require less practice time . . . like windsurfing.

Medley Relay*

This is a relay where the group competes against themselves or, more specifically, against a time or distance that they have previously established. In this case, total distance achieved by the group is the criterion.

Each member of the relay team must perform his/her best effort toward increasing the team's distance from a starting line. The performances are done in sequence; i.e., one after another, with each attempt being carefully marked and measured.

The events to choose from are as follows, but the sequence is up to you. I have found that finishing with the handstand walk provides an exciting finale. All of these events are measured from an initial starting line.

Medley Relay Events—(1) Standing broad (long) jump; (2) Standing backward jump; (3) Running long jump; (4) Cartwheel; (5) Dive and Roll; (6) One-legged hop (right and left leg); (7) Front forward flip from a stand; (8) Handstand walk. Add whatever type of forward movement that seems to make sense, or more appropriately, that is well received by the group. This is an activity that becomes more enjoyable through repetition.

68

Tree Soccer**

During an adventure curriculum workshop last summer, a group of us got together before dinner to play a bit of soccer. Teams were quickly arranged, but no one could agree on how large the goals should be, or where they should be located. A suggestion was made to use two large trees as the goals. The trees were about 40 yards apart on an otherwise open field. Here are the rules. The object (scoring a goal) is simply to hit the tree trunk (below 6 feet) with the soccer ball; all other soccer rules remain the same, with the following two exceptions: 1) There are no out-of-bounds. 2) After a score, the opposite team is allowed to make first contact with the ball from wherever it caroms after hitting the tree. Considering the above, it's apparent that there are no timeouts or stoppage of play—a very aerobic game.

Bump**

Bump is a bizzare indoor or outdoor game which has unusual co-ed implications associated with the action that develops. Be restrictive as to anatomical catching positions if you feel that your group is too immature to handle brief but sometimes suggestive juxtaposing of their bodies. Now that I have your interest, here are some rules and guidelines.

Working in teams of three, the object is to throw, catch, and transport a knotted towel or frisbee approximately 50 feet to an empty waste basket and deposit the towel into the container without letting it hit the floor. (On a warm day, and if your group's sense of humor allows, half fill the container with water.)

Divide the group into smaller groups of three, with one individual of the three acting as a thrower. Standing about 10-15 feet away from the two catchers, the thrower gently lofts a knotted towel toward his/her closely aligned partner. The two catchers must trap the towel without using their hands, arms, or shoulders, thus the name *Bump*. After catching it they must transport (hop, run, shuffle) the towel to the receptacle and deposit it within. If the towel is dropped en route to the container, the participants must run back and re-catch the towel.

After a successful deposit, the three teammates run back to the throwing area with their towel in hand, and the player roles are changed with one of the catchers becoming the thrower.

Play continues until the towel has been successfully plopped into the waste basket 3 times. The first group of three to finish wins the championship. Second, third, and fourth place are usually easy to judge, but as the cheering section increases there is a proportional decline in willingness to continue "Bumping" by the remaining players. No problem, everybody gets a ribbon in BUMP.

Blindfold Soccer*

Looking for a game that blends cooperation, trust, and communication—here 'tis.

Each team (two teams) tries to kick a ball past the end zone; no goal markers, just the line marking the end zone. A kick over the line scores a goal.

Divide the group into two equal teams (equal means numbers in this case because there's not much skill involved in sightless games). Each team divides into pairs and one member of each team puts on a blindfold.

Soccer rules act as a guide to establish parameters of play, but skills such as heading the ball, passing, trapping, are impractical at best. At this pre-game juncture, allow the pairs some practice time in "getting their act together." Let the sighted leader try leading by attempting to verbally guide his/her blindfolded partner around the field.

Game Time! Have both teams line up at opposite ends of the field. The action begins as a referee throws or kicks both balls onto the field in as neutral a manner as possible. Slightly deflated soccer-sized balls are used to reduce the distance a ball travels if kicked solidly.

Rules:

1. Only the blindfolded member of the pair can make physical contact with the ball. The sighted member can only offer verbal directions.

2. Members of the pair or groups of pairs are not allowed to purposefully touch one another. Normal game contact is OK as long as the touching is not of a directional type; i.e., pushing a blindfolded player toward the ball.

3. There are no goalies. This rule will make sense once the action begins. The word goalie and redundant in this case are synonymous.

4. If a ball is kicked beyond the sidelines, a referee will kick the ball back into play.

5. Do not allow and constantly warn against high kicks. No one knows when a kick is coming, so encourage a side-of-the-foot putting movement. Limiting high kicks is essential to safe play. If the players do not comply, stop the game: someone *will* get hurt otherwise.

6. Heavy boots are not allowed as instruments of shin destruction.

Considerations

1. There are two balls in play, which means that either ball can produce a goal. If the group is particularly large, use 3 balls as this tends to keep the players separated.

2. After one sightless group has stumbled around the field for a few minutes (or after a goal is scored) ask the players to trade roles. Give the new pair a chance to try out their command/reaction functions before starting again.

3. Teach the "bumpers up" position so that the blindfolded players have protection for the upper ventral part of their body. It's hands and arms up so that palms are forward and at about face height. Keep reminding the "blind" players to maintain this position.

Tube-e-Cide*

Tube-e-Cide is an exhausting field game that initially requires careful proctoring by the instructor in order to prevent unnecessary roughness during play. Once the rules are understood and followed, the game is a grand physical bash enjoyed by all.

The objects of play are two large truck inner tubes that, considering the popularity of tubeless tires, are becoming harder to find. When Tube-e-Cide is endorsed by the NCAA, I'm sure sanctioned game tubes will become readily available. For now, check out local tire discount stores for used tubes, even tubes with holes: patching is easy.

The object of the game is to score a goal by pushing or kicking your team's tube past and through the opposing team's goal posts. (Use a football field or your own goal markers.)

Divide the group (the more the better) into two equal teams and ask the players to go to opposite ends of the battle field. Place the two tubes on the 50 yard line, about 10 yards apart. Each tube needs an indentifying mark that can be easily recognized by the two teams. Use colored cloth strips (red and blue for example) to tie around the tubes, or spray paint a section of the tubes a distinctive color. Each team then chooses a runner to be blindfolded and a follow-up runner to provide directions.

At the signal GO, the two sightless runners start jogging from opposite ends of the field and, utilizing the verbal directions from their follow-up runner (no physical contact is allowed), attempt to be the first one to *their* tube. As soon as a blue runner makes contact with their tube, the entire blue team, waiting impatiently behind their respective goal line, runs onto the field and attempts to kick their tube toward the blue goal. The red team must remain behind the goal line until their runner has touched their tube. After initial contact is made with a tube, that runner may remove the blindfold.

Tube-e-Cide Rules

1. The first team to forward their tube over the goal line receives a point and all play stops. The tubes are set up on the mid-field line and play begins again as above.

2. The tube may be forwarded by any anatomical means (kick, push, knee) but cannot be touched with the hands.

3. Hooking is not allowed. (Putting your leg through the tube and attempting to hold the tube stationary.)

4. There are no boundaries and therefore no time outs.

5. There are no goalies per se.

6. Checking is allowed, but use of hands (pushing or grabbing other players) is not allowed. Females may not be checked, but, dynamic picks are OK.

7. To score a point the tube must enter the goal from the field side.

8. The penalty for unnecessary roughness is removal from the game.

Considerations

1. The more air in the tubes, the more action on the field.

2. Tubecide is suitable for all weather, but the ideal conditions produce a glazed snow surface for maximum action of the tubes.

3. Keep a patch kit and pump available for the inevitable small punctures that occur.

4. Use copious amounts of tape over the valve stem to prevent bare skin injury.

5. To handicap a group, give them a large tube. Small, highly inflated tubes travel much faster and farther when kicked.

6. Do not allow players to wear boots except in snowy conditions.

7. Tubecide on a soggy field is a dandy lead-up to mud wrestling.

8. Players should recognize that each team needs an offense and defense that operate concurrently and independently.

Pin Ball*

Pin ball provides the opportunity to use basketball skills without having to follow basketball rules or display any shooting capabilities. Playing on a basketball court, the object of *Pin Ball* is to knock over a guarded tennis can with a ball.

Method of Play and Rules:

Two co-ed teams distribute themselves randomly on the court. Two volleyballs or soccer balls (basketballs are too heavy) are put into play simultaneously by the referee. The balls should be thrown or kicked onto the court with no thought of direction or team affiliation.

A player must pass or dribble the ball toward the key area using the same rules that govern basketball, and try to knock over the "pin" by throwing or rolling the ball.

An empty tennis can or plastic soda container is placed in the center of the key (at both ends) and is guarded by a goalie; the only person allowed in the key circle. If anyone else on offense or defense steps inside the circle, the other team is awarded a point. The goalies may not step outside the circle or a point is given to the other team.

If a goalie accidentally knocks over his can, the opposing team gets the point. A goalie may not hold or adjust the can after play begins. No one is allowed to kick the goalies' can.

Both balls are collected and put into play by the referee after each score. Body-checking and other forms of physical contact are not allowed (basketball rules). The balls may not be kicked at any time by the players, although the goalie may use his/her feet to deflect a thrown ball. If penalties become necessary, figure out some unsavory consequence for the repeat offender.

For a change of pace and a lower score, use two goalies in each circle.

Outdoor Pin Ball

Try this game on a soccer or football field. Set up the goalie circles at each end of the pitch by either using chalk (lime) to form the circle or utilize a section of rope staked to the ground in a circle.

The balls are forwarded up and down the field by using *soccer* or *team hand ball* rules until a shot at the pin is made and then it's pure *Pin Ball*.

Night Exercises

If students are spending the night away from home at an outdoor education center or retreat and the evening hours are warm enough to support some nocturnal activity at your site, try these three feel-comfortable-with-the-dark games.

Don't limit these activities to just elementary-aged folks—I've experienced excellent results (positive feedback: "Hey, that was fun . . ." comments) from adults in adventure curriculum workshops.

Commandant**

The object of the first game is for one person (The Commandant) to keep all the rest of the players from making it back to home base in the dark. You will need one powerful flashlight and a portable home base. The portable home base isn't necessary, but it allows some flexibility in choosing game sites. An automobile makes a good home base. The field area that you choose for play should be free of rocks, stones and whatever else could put holes and dents in people.

The Commandant stands at the home base and counts to 50 slowly, while the rest of the players scatter to begin their nocturnal scamper back to home base, hopefully unseen. Each player must physically touch two large announced objects (tree, cabin) out in the field of play before they are allowed to try and get back to home base. These two objects must be in the Commandant's field of vision and at opposite ends of the field (at least 90 degrees apart).

The Commandant must turn on his/her light at the end of the 50 count, which visible action starts the game. Players, at this point, may be no closer than 10 yards to a mandatory touch object. The light can then be turned off or on as the Commandant chooses.

The Commandant may either stay near the base or roam far afield in order to try to catch someone. A catch is made if the Commandant spots someone and can call their name. At the initial stages of the game, a name must be used. Toward the end of the game, as people are dashing toward homebase, simply hitting a player with the light is enough for a "catch". A successful player, upon touching the home base, yells, FREE. A caught player walks back to home base and shares humorous insights with the growing numbers already there.

The first person to make it back FREE is the next Commandant, if the game is to be played again.

Considerations

Certain chances are being taken by playing this fast-moving game in the dark. Players move quickly with severely reduced vision, and although a certain amount of retinal adaptation takes place (night vision: a good teaching topic for an outdoor education center), there is still the chance that someone can trip and fall over or onto things that shouldn't be there, or run into unseen branches, etc. If you know the area (to be played in) well, the chances for injury are probably minimal, otherwise I'd have to recommend against this game.

The chance-taking on your part, as sponsor, group leader, etc., is the responsibility that you have as the decision-maker. Can this game be played safely within the parameters of the players' maturity level, the physical geography of the area, and whatever Murphy-like laws control each 24 hours?

Whooo?*

Another nighttime acclimatization game which allows a player to travel and/or hide alone in the dark without having to be very far from other players or home base . . . .

Ask for six volunteers to be hiders (ersatz owls, if you will). The number of hiders will vary as to the size of your group. Six hiders is sufficient for about 15 seekers. These folks hide in whatever wooded area avails itself in your camp location, recreation center, etc. The hiders try to pick a spot that allows their clothing to blend into the dark and shades of gray.

Each hider takes about a dozen identically numbered pieces of small paper with them, and heads for their chosen hiding spot. Giving the hiders a few minutes to situate themselves, the seekers begin their individual searches.

Each hider has the option to make a characteristic sound occasionally in order to help the searchers, particularly if no one is even getting warm (cold, warm, warmer, etc.—you know!). This compassionate rule is included to not only help the seekers, but gives the hider a role other than just hiding.

When a seeker actually makes contact with a hider, the found body soundlessly hands a numbered piece of paper to the discoverer. When a seeker has collected a predetermined number of slips or a particular numbered sequence, he/she can retire from the game and either watch the proceedings or try to confuse things with animal calls of their own.

The game helps younger players get used to the dark, and affords an engrossing evening activity that appeals to all ages.

No flashlights allowed. Make sure the hiders are well dressed if the temperature is cool. Sitting motionless in one place for a period of time is a good reminder (or lesson) of how physical activity helps to maintain body warmth.

75

A nocturnal hunt that sometimes shows things and people as they aren't. In an outdoor setting, split your group in half. Ask which group would like to be the outdoor hiders first. Take that chosen or volunteer half outside to a well-known or established trail, not far from the main cabin or building. The area along the trail should be partly cleared; i.e., not dense undergrowth. Visibility should be such that no street lamps or building lights can be seen.

Talk to the hiding group about how motionless objects (people) in the dark can take on other forms that appear to be rocks, stumps, logs. Indicate that as hiders they will want to cover all parts of their body that stand out (white skin or clothing), and camouflage body parts so that they blend into the surroundings. Then begin hiding members of the group along the trail following these rules and guidelines.

Hide people individually unless there is reluctance to stay alone and then, allow a pair to hide together.

A hider must be in a partially exposed position. Completely concealing a person behind something is not allowed. Try to blend the hider with the natural surroundings; a rock, tree stump, etc. A hider must be no more than 20 feet away from the trail.

The seekers wait patiently in the building until the leader of the hiding group comes back and announces that all is ready. Guidelines for seekers are as follows:

1. The object of the game is to find as many of the hiders as possible.
2. Point scores are kept for each team.
3. The seekers are taken to the trail head and told that from here on, they can expect to find hidden people on each side of the trail.
4. *The seekers may not leave the trail.*
5. When someone thinks they have spotted a hider, they call others over to have a look. If the concensus (vote?) is that there is actually someone there, the attending instructor shines his/her flashlight *directly* at the spot indicated by the seekers. If a hider is revealed, the seekers get a point. If there is no one there, the hiders get a point.

6. If all the seekers pass a hider on the trail, the instructor will call the group back and point out the hider with a flashlight. The hiders then get a point, and that particular hider can join the group and silently cheer on his/her group.

This procedure continues down the trail until the last hider has been found or is revealed. Points are added up to establish a nocturnal champion. The teams then reverse roles and the game is played again.

The reason that the seekers remain indoors until the hiders are set, is to show what a difference retinal adaptation (night vision) makes toward safe walking in the dark. In an outdoor education setting, this exercise is a natural lead into a discussion about the adaptations that nocturnal animals make toward existence in a reduced light environment: Mention bats, owls, cats.

I have personally led this game many times and can attest to its popularity. There is something exciting about being hidden only a few feet away from many probing eyes and remaining uncaught. Many of the hiders report that they heard strange noises as they waited silently for the seekers to reach their hopefully hidden area.

Do not allow any flashlights to be carried, except those held by an instructor.

Pick and Choose***

This is a grand initiative problem type of game that allows everyone to participate to the maximum of what they think they can do. You will need lots of used tennis balls.

Set three or four paper cores (or empty waste baskets) on a gym floor in the pattern represented below. Vary the placement and number of cores after you have tried the game a couple times.

The object of Pick and Choose is for a group (10-50) to try and throw as many tennis balls as possible into the cores during a two minute time period. Each core has a different point value, with the closest core scoring one point, the second 3 points, the third 5 points, and the farthest 9 points. The group is competing against itself in trying to score as high a point total as possible,

either by shuffling thrower and retriever positions or making a decision as to which cores should be targeted.

The group must now decide who are going to be throwers and who are going to be retrievers. The throwers must remain behind the throwing line. The retrievers may stand any place they wish, but they may not "help" the balls into the cores; their job is simply to retrieve missed shots and get the balls back to the throwers as fast as possible. Once the clock starts the throwers and retrievers may not exchange positions.

This is a decision-making game and should be played more then once so that the players can attempt to change their tactics and positions. Resist the temptation to make suggestions and let the action flow.

77

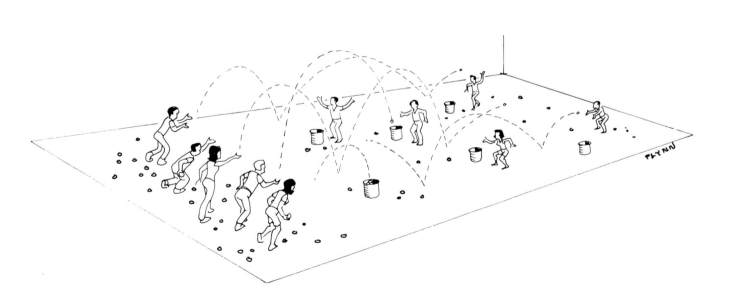

Count Coup***

Many moons ago, when Indian tribes warred against one another, honor and bravery often counted for more than ultimate physical victory on the field of battle. An Indian warrior, for example, could prove his bravery in combat by simply touching an opponent and voicing the words, COUNT COUP. Come to think of it, all conflicts would be more acceptable if battles were contemporarily fought in such a survivalist manner. However, if the surreptitiously touched opponent spun around and buried his hatchet in the head of the exulting and retreating brave, his COUNT COUP wouldn't count for much.

An ongoing game of *Count Coup* can be enjoyed in a camp or school setting (without the sanguinary consequences mentioned above: parents would complain) by establishing a few ground rules. *Count Coup* is not so much an imminent you-win-I-lose situation, but an ongoing, day-after-day, and in some cases, year-after-year, encounter of wits and memory between two or more consenting friends.

The game object is to touch a friend (concerns of anatomical areas can be assuaged by limiting touches to the appendages; i.e., arms and legs; more intimate COUPS are up to you), and say "Count Coup." Doesn't sound very exciting or ongoing does it? But if that friend or person is keenly aware that a COUP may be forthcoming at anytime and anywhere, then the ability to unselfconsciously keep a distance or remain "cool" at close quarters becomes essential and engrossing, particularly when you are both among a group of people that have no idea what is happening. This, then becomes the real game —knowing that a blatant, head-long attack would surely result in a COUP, but essentially recognizing that such a shallow victory would be unacceptable, and in fact counter to the unspoken rules of gamesmanship and fair play. Ah....the inherent satisfaction of lulling your opponent into a state of belief that your interest and intent are far removed from counting coup, and then subtly, inventively, and quietly making body contact, and uttering the words "count coup" at the same moment when the shock of "being had" registers on his/her face: that's COUP with panache, that transcends gaming, that's sneaky!

Count couping someone: in an elevator, on a stage, on their way to the bathroom at night, in a pool underwater are all well received COUP techniques. Couping by mail or note is in a different class, but entirely acceptable as long as the "on paper" rule has been established beforehand. And, for those of you who have played the game with me in the past. COUNT COUP! You know who. How sweet it is . . . .

78

BOY-O-BOY, DID WE EVER COUNT COUP!

FLYNN

Introduction to TRUST

Trust is a powerful and essential educational tool; it is the key to personal involvement. At the end of a semester in which adventure activities have been used, it's satisfying to hear students say "I'd like to try that," in contrast to their initial reaction of, "No Way!" A part of the reason for the extent of this growth in personal confidence is the establishment of trust. Trust that: I don't have to "do" everything; the safety equipment and procedures work; what the instructors say is honestly presented; if I try something and fail my peers will be supportive of my efforts; I will not be laughed at or made to appear foolish; my ideas and comments will be considered without ridicule.

An individual will seldom take a physical or emotional chance if they perceive callousness and unreasonable risk as part of that risk-taking. A group surrounded with positive experiences and successes will experience trust growing apace with personal confidence.

Trust, within the framework of an adventure curriculum, is gained with patience, thoughtfulness and care over a period of time, and can be damaged or lost in a second by carelessness or inconsiderate behavior. Cultivate and protect the trust that an individual offers and shares.

An effective and dramatic group trust exercise can be accomplished by asking a student to stand upon a stump, platform, ladder rung, etc., and fall backward into the arms of a prepared group of spotters. There should be at least 10-12 individuals standing on level ground to act as catchers. The platform should be 6 feet high or less.

The person falling should keep his/her arms held closely to the side of their body and fall with the body rigid; i.e., not bending at the waist. If the falling person does bend (pike) it concentrates the force of the fall to a small area (the posterior) and makes catching the bent faller more difficult.

The two lines of catchers stand shoulder-to-shoulder facing one another. Hands are extended palms up so that the hands are alternated and juxtaposed to form a secure landing area. Do not allow catchers, facing one another, to grasp hands or wrists in order to provide a firm, solid landing; knocked heads *will* result.

Assign one person in the group to stand on the platform with the volunteer about to fall. It's that person's responsibility to make sure the faller is: (1) spatially aligned with the catchers, (2) holding onto his/her pant seams tightly or with hands in pockets to prevent spontaneous flying elbows, (3) tilting his/her head back as a means of remaining rigid.

80

The platform proctor also should rearrange the spotters if it appears there is an appreciable strength or size discrepancy in opposing catchers. The proctor asks the catchers if they are ready and directs them to look up at the person about to fall. The fall follows immediately.

As an instructor, do not succumb to the temptation of being the first person to fall. The smiling, apparently confident group below you has probably never caught anyone before and the sight of a falling instructor, coupled with a novice's prerogative of doing everything wrong, might be enough to result in a very hard landing: not speculation, fact!

Place yourself in the catching line so that if everything goes wrong, you can either catch the falling volunteer by yourself or do a good job of slowing him/her down. After the students have caught a few fallers, remove yourself from the spotting line, keeping a close eye on what is happening.

If eventually the students say, "How come you haven't tried this yet; don't you trust us?" then it's time for your show of calculated confidence. If you are not planning to fall because you don't trust the students, then don't use this exercise. If you are working with a class of elementary age students and you are clearly too heavy for them

to catch, it's obvious that your choice to abstain has nothing to do with the students' lack of ability.

Try to have the participants alternate their position in the spotting line as different people take their turns at falling, so that all can eventually experience the responsibility of being a catcher. If you have a large group (20-40), it's clear that only a few students actually will be doing the catching at one time. To involve the entire group, ask the falling (fallen) person to continue holding himself/herself rigid so that he/she can be passed from hand to hand down the entire line of catchers. To further the commitment, ask the catchers to lift the faller to an overhead position for the trip down the line. Be aware that trust can be diminished as easily during this "hands on" passage as during the falling sequence. If a participant is dropped *at any time*, it will be awhile before the group, and particularly the dropped person, displays much enthusiasm toward future participation.

Appoint someone at the end of the line to be responsible for holding up the participant's torso while his/her feet are being lowered to the ground. Reversing this procedure is not met with much humor.

Make an attempt to achieve 100% participation during this activity, even if participation means simply standing on the platform and looking down at the line of catchers. From this point, "the position of potential," it's often easier to go ahead and fall than climb down. To quote from a former student who had been avoiding an attempt, "That's not fair, Karl. You know if I stand up there I'll do it."

On the other hand, very little is achieved by demanding that a student stay up there until he/she makes an attempt. Participation in this and all activities must result from the student's own decision and not because of the instructor's impelling personality and certainly not from any cute coercion tricks. Also, I feel that a student should not be left standing on a platform for more than a few minutes. The choice to perform or not should be entirely up to the participant, but a decision must be made to either go or not go after a reasonable period of time. The consequence of deciding to wait "until next time" is the mental anguish experienced in anticipation of that next time. The benefit of climbing down is that the student knows the activity is indeed voluntary and that his/her decision is being respected.

Contraindications:

There is a danger in beginning this activity from too high a platform. If the head and shoulders of the falling participant reach the catchers' hands before the feet, the platform is too high. A standing height of 7'-8' will produce this result. If some of the participants complain that the starting height is too high for them (even if it is only 4'-5') don't hesitate to offer them as low a starting height as necessary in order to include them in the activity. After some initial successes at a lower height they may then want to try a higher level. However, in your initial presentation, start with a challenging height; i.e., begin with a comparatively substantial challenge and then back off a bit for those who need an incremental series of boosts.

Ask for a volunteer to be the first one to fall. There always seems to be 2-3 individuals who want to try anything first, so as unobtrusively as possible, choose the lightest volunteer. There's little value in choosing El Gordo to provide an immediate and meaty challenge. Give the catching line some success before you release the 200+ pound DF (designated faller).

Ask all catchers and fallers to remove wrist watches and jewelry. Fallers should also remove keys, pencils, etc., from their pockets and large buckles from their belts.

Mention the potential dangers of using this activity "after hours." Doing a trust fall with friends after a couple of beers can result in physical and emotional disaster. Spinal cord injuries are forever.

Trust Dive

From a height of about 2'-4', ask a student to dive forward into the arms of 8-10 spotters. Ensure that the diving platform (stump, bleacher) is solid enough to preclude what we learned in Physics 101—the old "equal and opposite reaction to every action" . . . trick, namely, that the platform moves.

Indicate to the diver that he/she should aim for an invisible trapeze above the heads of the catchers, in order to land in an easily handled position: flat out, arms extended. Discourage dives, "into the pool" and pike position landings.

A set of bleachers provides a variable and usually solid take-off area. The diver can choose height and distance by moving up or down the bleacher steps. Other usable take-offs include, the back of a truck, a cut off tree stump, a low porch, and a well-positioned rock.

Arrange the catchers so that there is some

challenge to the dive, but not so close that the diver's movements are restricted by well-intentioned spotters. The position of the catchers is about the same as in the *Trust Fall* activity with the exception that the spotters' bodies are turned halfway toward the diver with one foot moved toward the center of the catching line. This oblique body orientation provides more ability to absorb the momentum of the diver.

To increase the commitment of the diver, remove the first two spotters; i.e., increase the distance from the diver to the spotters. Let this be a choice that the diver makes. Choosing to remove the first and sometimes second pair of spotters is not as dramatic a move as it seems initially. A diver will probably not make such a decision unless he is sure of the outcome; and even if the dive comes up short, only the diver's feet will drag on the ground.

Falling Down Without Going BOOM

There are several reasons for including how-to-fall instructions as part of growing up, not the least of which is achieving that goal. Learning to fall is basic training that should be required learning for children, because most people (children and adults) don't know how to handle a fall effectively in order to minimize or eliminate injury. Unfortunately many children grow up in such a protected sphere that the chance to learn day-to-day survival skills never materializes. "Be careful!" "Don't get hurt!"; have become less of a mother's hopeful entreaty and more of a not-to-be-ignored parental demand. Learning to fall:

1. . . . increases the safety margin for participants in risk-oriented activities, such as soccer, bicycle riding, ropes courses, and walking to school.
2. . . . decreases the possibility of injury as the result of a fall.
3. . . . develops increased confidence in one's physical and psychological ability to overcome problem situations.

Injury resulting from forward or backward moving falls usually is caused by friction on the palms and body (abrasions), or by the sudden absorption of the shock with the hands (sprained or broken wrists).

The falling and rolling technique described here reduces the potential for injury. Confidence that a fall can be handled safely also results in an increased personal commitment to attempt tasks or games where there is some risk of a moving fall.

A proven way to escape or minimize injury in a moving fall is to use a modified forward or backward shoulder roll. The shoulder roll is spontaneously initiated as the result of a fall combined with some forward or backward movement (trip, push, jump); otherwise the roll aspect is comically superfluous. A direct jump down from a height can be accomplished safely (depending upon the height, of course) if the shock of the fall is taken with the legs and a lesser amount by the hands and arms.

There are times when the difference between a short fall and possible injury is an effective spotter.

Spotting itself involves having one or more individuals in position to "catch" an off-balance participant. The spotter(s) must learn to recognize that catching means to support the upper part of the body, with most concern being directed toward the head. I'm sure some folks feel that other parts of their anatomy are as important, but for the sake of a sentient existence, let's stick with the cranium. Literally catching (superman style) the mass of a falling body is difficult and dangerous and may result in injury to both parties.

Emphasize constant attention to the performers and attempt to anticipate their movements. A good spotter is the result of actual training, not of reading or being lectured about spotting. It is hard to believe how rapidly a person can switch from a balanced posture 6 feet off the ground to a prone position on the ground. A realistic demonstration by the instructor helps to emphasize the attentiveness necessary to be an effective spotter.

Use spotters generously when the situation indicates their need. Avoid, however, using so many ultra-concerned spotters that they get in each other's way or, in some cases, actually prevent the participant from falling off a low cable. Give the participant a chance to succeed or fail; just be there if the failure results in an out-of-control fall.

That elusive feeling of trust that develops gradually within a group can be easily diminished or lost by horseplay or inattentiveness. Guard against these lapses, recognizing that it takes longer to redevelop group trust than to establish it in the first place.

To guage the initial proficiency level of the group, ask the students to form a semi-circle facing the instructor and in turn demonstrate a forward or backward fall and roll. You may be appalled at how many students cannot perform this simple movement. Watch for well intentioned and uncoordinated attempts that could result in injury. Having the students demonstrate a shoulder roll one-by-one allows the instructor to provide individual attention (albeit brief) and to make critical comments from which everyone can benefit.

The individual attitude that you are trying to establish is, "I'll be anxious about trying something new, but not overly concerned with failure because of the supportive nature of my group."

Front Roll Practice

Demonstrate falling forward from a standing or squatting position and continue into a front shoulder roll. The roll can be initiated either to the right or left, depending upon the force causing the fall, or the side which is most natural for the faller.

If rolling on the right shoulder, the left hand is put out as a guide (not a brace). The right hand (palm down) and arm are extended in front of the individual. The elbow is slightly bent as the right forearm provides a surface for the beginning of the roll. The performer looks under his left armpit, thus ensuring that the head is in the proper position, and continues a forward rolling movement onto the right shoulder in tuck position and finally into a squat position. The actual roll is neither straight over (somersault) nor a lateral roll, but rather a forty-five degree combination.

Back Roll Practice

The legs begin to bend as the body turns slightly toward the hip that is going to have first contact with the ground. Hands guide the tucked body as the roll is completed over the shoulder on the same side as the hip that made first contact.

The front and back roll can be practiced first from a standing (or squatting) position and eventually, as practice and skill allow, from a jog or slow run.

Fall and Roll Exercises

1. The group lines up on the goal line of a football field facing toward the other goal. About 6-8 feet distance between students is necessary for safety. On a signal, the participants begin a series of forward fall-and-rolls up to the 25 yard line. After attempting this two or three times in consecutive class sessions, ask students to see how few rolls it requires to reach the 25 yard marker. Front and back rolls can be alternated for this distance; i.e., front roll, pivot; back roll, pivot; front roll, etc.

Measure and cut an appropriate number of 3 foot lengths of clothesline. Have the students tie the line around their own ankles with a simple any-do-it knot. With the feet securely tied together, the students attempt a front and back shoulder roll. Having the feet tied together initiates a functionally proper roll, since the legs are forced to stay together during execution.

2. Line up one half of the group facing the other half at approximately arm's length. Explain that a more spontaneous fall and roll can be accomplished if the fall is initiated by someone other than the faller. A two-handed compassionate shove at the shoulders (partners alternating shoves) will accomplish this "spontaneous" acceleration.

3. To alleviate foolishness and possible injury from too forceful a shove, the push should be delivered on command. Beforehand, demonstrate what you consider to be a reasonable two-handed push.

4. Jumping and rolling from a height can be attempted after the roll itself is mastered. The jumps are attempted at gradually increasing heights (one foot increments if possible) until a height of five or six feet is reached. Critique the rolls carefully, and if necessary limit some students from increasing height until their technique is improved.

5. If a less intimidating fall and roll is indicated for some individuals, have those students assume a squat position and then lean forward into a shoulder roll. After accomplishing this movement with some semblance of agility, suggest that the student leap-frog forward from this squat position, and shoulder roll into another identical squat position. This physically pleasing movement sequence can be strung together to produce a leap-roll-leap-roll exercise.

6. If the group has achieved a reasonable proficiency level in jogging and falling, and the ground isn't frozen, try the following SPECTACULAR.

Ask the group to line up at the end of a field. Explain that they will be jogging up and down the field together, changing direction and body orientation on command. At the signal FALL, everyone must fall and roll from whatever position he/she is in at that moment. Try to initiate the falls from odd body positions to emphasize that falling is not always experienced in an ideal position.

Twice up and down the field is sufficient for practice and still remains within the realm of fun.

7. The following dramatic exercise can serve as a culmination to the fall and roll training.

Ask the group to form a flanking line facing away from you with their eyes closed. Require a distance of about five feet between students. Indicate that you are going to walk behind the line and initiate a fall by delivering a push at their shoulders. Assure any students who do not want to participate that they are free to step aside (although very few will, at this point).

Walk quietly behind the line and deliver controlled pushes to shoulder blades. The students are anticipating the shove, so little pressure is required to initiate the fall. Shove randomly so that the students don't know when their turn is coming.

There is a paradoxical and gleeful push me/don't push me feeling associated with the anticipation. Actually, this "graduation" exercise is more fun than functional.

Consideration

Participants who continue to experience trouble with the basic shoulder roll often feel compelled (self and peer pressure) to try the more advanced fall and roll stunts before they are ready, and injury results. It's ironic, but unfortunately true, that a person can get hurt while training to avoid injury. It's part of your role to identify those individuals who need more practice and support.

Sherpa Walk **

This follow-the-leader, action-oriented walk is probably the longest duration trust activity (other than marriage) that I've taken part in. It is also a fine activity for developing communication, no matter how outlandish the message means become.

You will need a blindfold for each participant.

1. Cut the blindfolds long enough so that tying them around the head doesn't become an initiative problem.

2. Offer *clean* blindfolds for hygienic and humanitarian reasons.

3. Use cloth that does not admit light, or else cloth that can be doubled.

4. Have more cloth on hand than you anticipate needing.

Ask the entire group (8 - no more than 15) to tie on blindfolds. If you have not previously mentioned the trust aspects of participating in a blindfolded activity, those comments would be appropriate at this juncture. To wit, the instructor will not make fun of anyone, or make anyone appear to be foolish because of being blindfolded. (Such trite shenanigans are usually not funny, and the loss of confidence certainly is not worth a shallow bit of humor.)

You need to relate a story line that gives this upcoming sightless bash some reason for being. Use the following slice of fantasy as an outline to develop your own patter.

"Your travelers' group has elected to tour an exotic and politically forbidden area of the Asian continent. The charter flight, aboard Xanth Airlines, was difficult to obtain (visa problems) and prohibitively expensive. However, because of personal wealth and governmental leniency, the plane and your group has arrived in the country of Ultimo Sotto Voce to the strains of their national anthem; a 12-note dirge in 4/4 time repeated in endless succession. The reason for the appropriateness of this metronome-like anthem is that all the people in USV are deaf (very small and insular country—inbreeding and all that), and they wouldn't appreciate a longer or more varied melody: they like the beat. Considering their removed location on the continent (with resultant limited exposure to other people), it would come as no surprise that

PLYNN

their meager language (actually, almost a complete lack of phonetic communication: 2 vowels, 5 consonants) is incomprehensible to your group.

"Sadly, about a decade ago, the populace became endemically afflicted with leprosy as the result of the unlikely situation of a Polynesian immigrant's having introduced the disease via an aborted airline hi-jack and resultant emergency parachute attempt (refer to page 1 story in Leahali Gazette, Nov. 14, 1969 — "Leaping Leper Leaves Legacy"), etc., etc., etc.

The Problem - After having lightheartedly presented the background information, tell your blindfolded travelers that two Sotto Voce citizens will lead them blindfolded through a sacred area to where the tour bus will pick them up.

Lightly tap two members of the group on the head (SV tour guides) and tell them to come with you so that you can point out the route through the sacred ground. Explain to the remainder of the group that you will return within five minutes and that they should take this time to arrange themselves in some way for sightless traveling.

Take your two chosen leaders (blindfolds now off) and point out a preselected route through which you would like them to lead the group. Spend some time, prior to the group's initial meeting, to establish a challenging and enjoyable route. Include: bashing through some bushes, having to crawl under and over something, walking next to water (which you can splash threateningly), passing over and down a 6-7 foot drop-off, etc.

Explain to the leaders (and eventually the group) that they are not allowed to say anything (language, inflections) that the group will understand, but can make whatever other sounds they like: whistles, clucking, clapping, etc. Guides are not allowed to touch any members of the group (leprosy—remember?). So, obviously, a means of communication must be established in a minimum amount of time. Give the leaders a couple of minutes to discuss communication stategies while you walk back

and explain the situation to the now highly organized (?) travelers.

Assure the group that you and one other proctor will be silently attending this walk to provide spotting in case of any potentially risky moves. As you see the leaders approach, say "The next semi-human sounds you hear will come from your Sotto Voce leaders."

As you walk along, with what becomes a very verbal group of travelers, watch for potential danger and put yourself in a good spotting position if necessary. Most people are unhesitatingly trusting and will walk off a cliff if pointed in that direction. Temper challenge with compassion. Point out the route to the leaders if they seem lost. Watch and listen for situations that will be valuable to relate during the post-session discussion.

Try to end up the walk in an area that allows the group to be physically close together. After you announce that they have arrived at the "bus terminal" (blindfolds can be removed), and the initial exclamations of "Where are we?", etc., have been made, ask the leaders to walk the group back through the route to satisfy their curiosity and allow spontaneous sharing of reactions and sensations. Finish up with a sit-down debriefing session.

Yeah, But....*

Here's an action-oriented way to develop trust within a group. Blindfolds will be necessary for most folks.

Ask an individual to stand at one end of a basketball court, with his/her back to the wall. Have that person assume the hands-up/palms out, protect-yourself position (bumpers up). At this juncture, the individual is either blindfolded or has committed to keep his/her eyes closed. Ask the participant to *jog* toward the far wall at a steady, unchanging pace.

The remainder of the group is spread out in a flanking line with their backs to the wall that the blindfolded jogger is approaching. The job of these spotters is to stop the jogger before he/she encounters, vis-a-vis, the wall.

The results are impressive, and students generally choose to try it more than once. This activity provides an action-oriented preliminary to the trust fall.

Don't allow *any* fooling around by the spotters; trust is a fragile commodity and is easily broken. Ask the spotters to be as quiet as possible in order to increase the commitment of the jogger.

Place a few spotters about ¾ of the way down court on the sidelines to prevent wildly disoriented joggers from smacking into the bleachers or wall. Don't ignore this suggestion; it happens.

91

PLYNN

This "hands on" group activity is an old outdoor education standby that can be used effectively in an adventure program. It can be presented to two ways.

Ostensibly, the object is for the group to audibly experience the sounds of a summer rain approaching and leaving an area. If the group cooperates and performs their individual roles well, there is the distinctly rewarding experience of hearing the increasing wind, the pitter-patter of rain drops and eventual heavy drumming sounds of a brief rainstorm. But the greatest benefit results from achieving the cooperation and trust level that is necessary for the elements to be realistically heard and felt.

Ask your group (any number up to 50) to make a circle and then turn to their right (or left, it doesn't matter). Have them close up the circle by side-stepping toward the center of the circle until they can easily touch the person's back in front of them. Explain that the group is going to try and experience (tactually and audibly) the rain shower mentioned above, and that their utmost cooperation is needed for this to happen.

Using the person in front of you (*you* are part of the circle), demonstrate the movements necessary to achieve the sounds desired as follows:

1. With your palms flat on the person's back (shoulders) in front of you, make a rotating movement with your hands to achieve a swishing sound (the increase of wind preceding a shower).

2. Change to a slapping motion with your finger tips on your partner's back (beginning rain drops).

3. Change to a heavier finger slapping action (harder rain drops).

4. Return to the motions of #2.

5. Return to the motions of #1.

6. STOP, and wait for all sounds to cease. When you begin #1, at the onset of this exercise, your partner passes along the motion to the person in front of them and so on until the motion is returned to you; i.e., feeling the hand rotation on your back; at which point you begin #2 and so on until the end.

This exercise is much more effective if the group decides to keep their eyes closed for the duration of the "coming and going of the rain."

Pick your location for this group action with some forethought. Do not ask a group of students to try this sensitive sequence with other people wandering by, and try to pick a spot that is as quiet as possible—no lawnmowers or chain saws to interrupt the emotionally fragile sound sequence that you are trying to build.

If your group can't handle the touch that is required in the former method, place yourself in the center of the circle and have everyone face toward you. Ask the group to follow your lead, and you change the sounds when it seems appropriate. Unfortunately in this case, the sounds do not meld into one another, but it's still an effective experience.

The sounds are made by:
1. Rubbing your palms together.
2. Snapping your fingers alternately.
3. Snapping multi fingers.
4. Slapping your thighs.
5. Pounding your chest and reverse the order.

Squat Thrust **

This is a low center of gravity variation of an old one-on-one activity called *Stand Off*, in which two people faced one another and tried to knock each other off balance by striking their palms against one another. If either player moves a foot, they lose. An effective strategy is not to always try to make contact with the other player's palms, but to occasionally fake a thrust in order to make the opponent lose his/her balance.

In *Squat Thrust* the rules and strategy are essentially the same, but the players assume a more precarious balanced position by squatting in front of one another so that the balance point is on the ball of the foot. The contests do not last as long and the results of being knocked off balance are more entertaining. The contest is a functional preliminary activity for use with the Slo-Mo exercise.

Slo–Mo **

Try this slow motion sequence as a cooperative/strength exercise for two participants. With a partner (same size or sex isn't necessary), stand toe-to-toe and palm-to-palm. Each participant tries to maneuver his/her partner off balance (without moving either foot) by pushing against each other's palms in *slow motion* only. No fast moves are allowed, even to gain an advantage or win. The two contestants become cooperative partners, tempering competitive urges with knowledge that compassion and cooperation are necessary to make the activity "work." It feels good to win, but it also feels good to cooperate with a former competitor. There is more feel to this exercise than explanation allows. Try it.

Most contests conveniently end with both folks simultaneously losing (winning?); i.e., falling off balance together.

Initiative Problems

Initiative exercises offer a series of clearly and often fancifully defined problems. Each task is designed so that a group must employ cooperation and some physical effort to gain a solution. Some problems are more cerebral than physical and vice-versa.

This problem-oriented approach to learning can be useful in developing each individual's awareness of decision-making, leadership, and the obligations and strengths of each member within a group. Participants engage the problem in groups to take advantage of the combined physical and mental strengths of a team. These initiative problems also can be employed to promote an individual's sense of his own competence, and they also serve to help break down some of the stereotypes which exist so comfortably in our social network. Finally, initiative problems are a nonpareil for building morale and a sense of camaraderie.

Presenting Group Initiative Problems

Teachers and instructors should be familiar with these basic guidelines for initiative problem presentation.

(1) Choose a problem suited to the age and physical ability of the group. An older group is easily turned off by a childish situation, and any group quickly becomes frustrated by a problem that requires physical or mental skills beyond their capabilities.

(2) Find a safe and convenient place to set up the problem and make use of existing materials and supports (trees, poles, etc.) whenever possible.

(3) Make all the rules and procedures clear to the participants before they attempt the problem. Avoid overwordiness and too many rules.

(4) Present the situation and rules, then step back and allow the group to work (and sometimes stumble) through the problem. While the instructor sets up the problem, and probably knows the best way to solve it, very little good will come from interrupting the problem-solving process by giving hints or indicating to the participants a more efficient or "right" way. Interaction is the important process which takes place during an initiative problem, not how well the participants are performing physically under the established guidelines.

(5) Initiative problems may be presented in as many different ways as instructor personalities and intuition allow. Some present a highly fanciful situation (the poison peanut butter crowd) while others present the situation exactly as it is. Select a method of presentation which is comfortable for you, and suitable for the particular group.

(6) As the group attempts to complete the initiative problem, situations may arise when a participant will (usually inadvertently) break a ground rule, thus making the completion of the problem a fairly easy matter. The penalty for such an infraction can be either a time penalty or starting the problem over. Whether to employ penalties and the extent to which they are used depend upon the instructor's approach.

Be strict in administering the rules of the problem. If the group suspects that you don't care about following the rules (the framework of these fabrications), the problem will dissolve into horseplay and become functionally meaningless.

(7) For variety, initiative problems may occasionally be presented as a timed, competitive exercise in order to increase interest and individual effort. Such competition usually takes one of two forms: (a) having the group members compete against themselves, in order to improve on a previous record;

(b) setting up a competition against other groups or against a time limit.

Timed competition against a nebulous group from a school in Western Wherever seems to work toward providing a goal to shoot for. Negative competition, within this framework of positive cooperative effort, results from the old redbird vs. bluebird situations, where there must be a tangible winner and loser.

(8) If you are working with a group of about 25-30, it will probably make sense to split the group in half for participation in games or initiative problems. If too many people are involved, ideas and good intentions may be shunted aside in favor of loudness and individual popularity.

(9) After a group has completed (or tried to complete) a problem, the details should be discussed by all who were involved. The discussion should focus on the process the students have just experienced. They can examine what decisions were made and by whom; who had ideas that were not expressed, or that were expressed but not heard or listened to. The discussion also may focus on the roles of males and females, students and adults, athletes and scholars, etc. The conversations may move naturally into a comparison of the cooperative processes which characterize school life or of our society in general.

Verbalization of the group's experience and reaction to a common task is often enlightening to the group and to the instructor.

As instructor you were obliged, during the problem-solving process, to be silent. Now, in your role as facilitator, you get the chance to carefully pick and choose your comments and those moments when an insightful word or two are best offered. Keep the conversations flowing with pertinent remarks, topics of discussion, and well-chosen humorous vignettes. Use the following list of debriefing topics. These discussion topics offer lead-in keys in order to get the most from a group sharing session.

Initiative Problem Debriefing Topics

Leadership & Followership
Chiefs & Indians; how many and what's necessary?
Group Support
What is it? Where does it come from?
Peer Pressure
Negative or positive effect?
Negativism-Hostility
How do you handle it? Why is it there?

Efficiency
The step beyond just doing it.
Competition
Against self, teams, a nebulous group or record
Spotting
Why essential?
Sexism
Who plays what role?
Carry Over
Do these fabricated problems have real life significance?
Fear, Physical & Psychological
Fear of height? Failure? Looking bad?
Joy - Pleasure
At the heart of it all - the raison d'etre.

When leading a discussion it is a good idea to have the students sit so that they can see everyone else in the group. Ask the students to agree not to interrupt the speaker, and not to put down or to ridicule anyone else's ideas or comments. Make sure everyone knows that he/she has the right to pass (remain silent) in any discussion. The teacher's goal is to establish a supportive group rapport so that individuals won't feel intimidated or frightened to say what's on their minds.

96

98

I probably use this activity more than any other get-to-know-you sequence. Hog Call is a grand excuse to make a lot of unselfconscious noise and is a nifty means of "breaking the ice" with a just-met group.

Ask any size group to make a line facing you, standing shoulder-to-shoulder so that the oldest person (to the nearest day) is to your left, and the youngest person is to your right. This mix-up usually involves a lot of talking, age disclaimers, and laughter; s'ok, you're on the right track. Encourage this banter and exchange of jibes, particularly among those folks to your left.

After the line is established, take a minute to establish a median age for the group (to also allow the badinage some wind-down time) and establish if there were any birthdays occuring in the same year? month? day? who knows, with something in common, two people might even talk to one another—stranger things have happened.

Ask the younger end of the line to fold around and walk toward the other end of the line so that the youngest ends up facing the most venerable. (The oldest, but you don't have to say that.) Each person should have a face-to-face partner. Ask everyone to shake hands with the person opposite them to make sure that each individual is part of a pair.

Explain that you would like each pair to share a matching set of words or sounds; e.g., shoe-foot, buzz-ball, peanut-butter, whiskey-sours. In addition, each person should choose one of the words or sounds as theirs. You will soon see why this distinction is important. Ask each pair to announce their choice in order to enjoy the humor of the more inventive selections, and more specifically to make sure there are no duplications.

Indicate that each line represents a group that will soon move to opposite ends of a gym, field, parking lot. Then ask each member of the pairs to walk to opposite ends of the field with the instructions that they are to put on blindfolds when they arrive. The object of the imminent action is to find their word partner, and since everyone is blindfolded, the most functional means would seem to be verbal. Right! So, each participant shouts their partner's word/sound in order to pair up. For example, if I'm PEANUT, I would *yell* BUTTER over and over until my partner and I become PEANUT-BUTTER. Choose one of the participant's words and shout it as loudly as you can to demonstrate what type of volume is expected. Experience shows that if you want someone or a group to perform an action that is potentially embarrasing or difficult, you better be ready to try it yourself.

After the blindfolds are on, ask the participants to mill around to keep them from eyeballing their partner at a distance—a bit of inevitable gamesmanship. Also teach the "bumpers up" position; i.e., hands up and palms forward, in order to provide personal protection while moving sightlessly around. Assure everyone that you will prevent them from going too far astray or from walking into something (other people excluded; that's what the "bumpers" are for).

When pair members finally find one another, amidst a cacophony (particularly indoors) of shouted sounds, ask the seekers and finders to remove their blindfolds and share with one another the following: names, where they are from, and perhaps why they came to this particular clinic. (Before getting into a heavy dialogue, it's fun to look at the name-shouting crowd around you; unless you happen to be the last noisy couple.) Let one-on-one conversations happen for about 5-10 minutes, depending upon how well things seem to be going. Then retire with the group to a comfortable spot (no

mosquitos, lawnmowers, sun-in-their-eyes, etc.) and, sitting in a circle, ask any person to begin the sharing by introducing their partner. When that individual has finished saying whatever seems appropriate, their partner reciprocates the introduction. That second person then chooses another member of a pair, hopefully by name, and the introductions continue.

As the facilitator, interject appropriate comments if necessary to keep the comments flowing and perhaps to help a nervous participant, but otherwise sit back and enjoy the repartee.

If you are in a location where loud shouting would be disruptive or offensive, try the whisper method. Ask the players to find each other, using the same rules as above, by whispering their words or sounds. It's ludicrous, functional, and funny.

99

Everybody Up ***

Using this initiative exercise is a useful way to introduce the concept of group cooperation.

Ask two people of approximately the same size to sit on the ground (gym floor) facing one another so that the bottoms of their feet are opposed, knees are bent, and hands are tightly grasped. From this stylized sitting position, ask the duo to try and pull themselves into an upright standing position. If the pair is successful (most are), ask them to seek another partner and try standing up with three people, then four, etc., until the entire group eventually makes an attempt. Criteria for a successful attempt are: 1) Hands grasped so that an electrical current could pass through the group, 2) Foot contact with the same electrical set-up, 3) All derrieres off the ground at the same time.

Something that began as a simple cooperative stunt becomes an initiative problem that includes the entire group.

An expanding group will soon find that the seemingly logical circular configuration of bodies cannot be continued beyond 8 or so. A change of thinking (initiative) must be employed to come up with a solution that allows large numbers (50 people or more) to complete the problem.

If an adrenalin-pumped group of 8 or 10 jogs over to you, after having stumbled and jerked to a tenuous standing position, and breathlessly asks, "Did we do it right?"—need I say what your answer should be? Are they high? Yes. Do they feel good about their effort and themselves? Yes. Did they do it right?

An alternate or additional way to present this problem is to ask the participants to sit back-to-back and try to stand as a pair, a trio, etc. Do not allow interlocked arms for safety reasons (shoulder dislocation possibilities).

Peter Steele

Ice Breakers **

This activity provides an initiative "ice breaker" task for a group of people that have just met one another and will be working together in the future.

Object:

a.) to learn something about each person in the group,

b.) to unselfconsciously relate something unusual about yourself,

c.) to perform a task together,

d.) to begin learning names.

Procedure:

Tie a rope around the entire clustered group so that the rope is looped tightly enough to hold the people closely together but not so constricting that moving or breathing becomes a problem. Use at least half a dozen turns of rope to give the group a feeling of being actually tied together.

After the rope is in place, ask the group to make its way from point A to point B, and while attempting this task, to have each person relate something about him/herself which is unusual or of which he/she is particularly proud. The route should be carefully chosen to offer occasional physical obstacles that are easy enough to preclude frustration, but difficult enough to offer the group some satisfaction (fun) in having overcome them together. For example: Up or down stairs, through a loose hedge, over a curb, around tight corners.

It should be explained that after all the shuffling, squeezing, and bumping, the group will be responsible for remembering what each individual has briefly related about him/herself, and his/her first name.

After the group has completed the task, retire to a comfortable spot (untied) and elicit responses from the participants by pointing to each individual separately and asking the group what that person has done that is unusual that he/she is proud of having done. Generally the responses are humorous and nearly 100% correct. This is a fun-oriented activity. Match your approach toward this goal.

A Variation:

Another way to arrange this task is to first ask the group to line up according to age (this works well in a workshop situation but not with a high school group). Ask the line to fold in half so that each person is facing another person (most venerable facing youngest, etc.). During the obstacle portion of the "ice breaker" walk, these people pairs are responsible for learning something unusual about one another so that after the problem is completed, each member of the pair can introduce the other to the group and relate whatever off-beat tidbits about his/her partner that he/she has learned.

Or, rather than asking the initial line to fold in half (as mentioned), ask the most venerable person to begin slowly rotating, thus wrapping the remainder of the line around him/herself. This winding rotation produces a large, tightly coiled spiral that can then be further solidified by wrapping and tying with a rope. The spiral (a snail, perhaps) can then (snail-like) move off to accomplish its task. Ask people with stiff-soled boots to be careful of less protected toes.

To make the task a bit more difficult and ludicrous, ask the group to start and end in a seated (bottoms on the ground) position.

101

WORDLES **

Printed onto 3″x5″ cards, WORDLES provide an interesting and enjoyable series of unique word puzzles which serve as the basis for lively group discussions. It is a rainy day special that encourages brainstorming and rapid-fire comments. Try a few yourself; they become infectious.

Sample use—Show your participants a series of WORDLES and provide answers if necessary to establish a directional thinking process. Then divide the group into subgroups of 3-5. Give each of these smaller groups a series of six 3″x5″ cards, face down. Explain that each card contains a different WORDLE. Each group might have the same WORDLES, but not necessarily in the same order.

On a signal the group turns up one card at a time and tries to figure out the meaning of the letters. This group effort is timed. As soon as a WORDLE is deciphered, the group turns immediately to the next card, but they must stay with a problem WORDLE for two minutes before moving on.

The shortest final time recorded means ...; you pick the award or temporary title.

Try to stimulate the groups to make up their own WORDLES. Once you start thinking ndsıpə poʍu and o

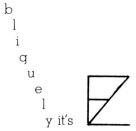

b
l
i
q
u
e
l
y it's

102

1. SIDE SIDE

2. YOU/JUST/ME

3. BAN ANA

4. ONCE / A TIME

5. *NOON LAZY*

6. DEAL

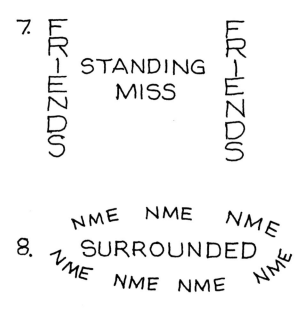

7. FRIENDS STANDING MISS FRIENDS

8. NME NME NME SURROUNDED NME NME NME NME NME

9. ECNALG

10. $\dfrac{2\,UM}{+2\,UM}$

11. HO

12. HIJKLMNO

13. TIME
   ABDE

14.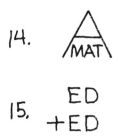

15. $\dfrac{ED}{+ED}$

16. TIMING TIM ING

17. MCE
   MCE
   MCE

18. WHEATHER

19. ME NT

20. ALL WORLD

21. DIS O HES
   $\overset{M}{\underset{M}{\text{DISO HES}}}$

22. IECEXCEPT

23. BJAOCKX

24. HAND

25. PAS

26. AGO

27. YOUR PaAnNtTsS

28. GESG

29. ONE
   ONE

30. ISSUE ISSUE
   ISSUE ISSUE
   ISSUE ISSUE
   ISSUE ISSUE
   ISSUE ISSUE

31. NAFISH
   NAFISH

32. _____ IT

33. STOMACH

34. PROMISES

35. LAL

103

36. MOTH
CRY
CRY
CRY

37. ME QUIT

38. $\dfrac{O}{\text{M.D.}}$
Ph.D.
L.L.D

39. ii ii
O O

40. $\dfrac{\text{STAND}}{\text{I}}$

41. DICE
DICE

42. O - 144

43. CYCLE
CYCLE
CYCLE

44. KNEE
LIGHT

45. GROUND
FEET
FEET
FEET
FEET
FEET
FEET

46. HE'S/HIMSELF

47. DOCTOR
DOCTOR

48. K
C
E
H
C

49. R
ROAD
A
D

50. ++

51. THHAENRGE

104

Answers to WORDLES:

1. Side by side
2. Just between you and me
3. Banana split
4. Once upon a time
5. Lazy afternoon
6. Big deal
7. Misunderstanding between friends
8. Surrounded by enemies
9. Backward glance
10. Forum
11. Half an hour
12. Water (H to O)
13. Long-Time-No-See
14. Matinee
15. Added
16. Split second timing
17. Three blind mice
18. A bad spell of weather
19. Apartment
20. It's a small world afterall
21. Mom breaking dishes
22. i before e except after c
23. Jack-in-the-box
24. Hand in hand
25. Incomplete pass
26. Long ago
27. Ants in your pants
28. Scrambled eggs
29. One-on-one
30. Tennis shoes
31. Tuna fish
32. Blanket
33. Upset stomach
34. Broken promises
35. All mixed up
36. Mothballs
37. Quit following me
38. Three degrees below zero
39. Circles under the eyes
40. I understand
41. Paradise
42. O—gross
43. Tricycle
44. Neon light
45. Six feet under ground
46. He's beside himself
47. Paradox
48. Check up
49. Cross road
50. Double cross
51. Hang in there

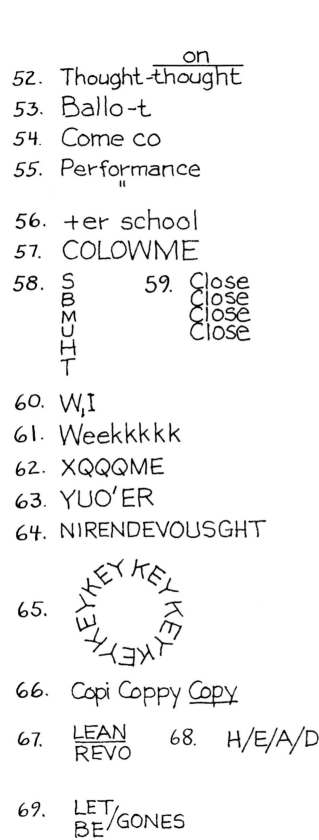

52. Thought ~~thought~~ (on)
53. Ballo-t
54. Come co
55. Performance "
56. +er school
57. COLOWME
58. S
    B
    M
    U
    H
    T
59. Close
    Close
    Close
    Close
60. W,I
61. Weekkkkk
62. XQQQME
63. YUO'ER
64. NIRENDEVOUSGHT
65. KEYKEYKEY KEY (arranged in ring)
66. Copi Coppy Copy
67. LEAN
    REVO
68. H/E/A/D
69. LET/GONES
    BE

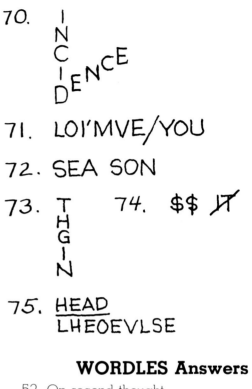

WORDLES Redux

70. I
    N
    C
    I   NCE
    D E
    D
71. LOI'MVE/YOU
72. SEA SON
73. T
    H
    G
    I
    N
74. $$ ~~IT~~
75. HEAD
    LHEOEVLSE

105

WORDLES Answers

52. On second thought
53. Absentee ballot
54. There's more to come
55. Repeat performance
56. Summer school
57. Low income
58. Thumbs up
59. Foreclose
60. I'm upset
61. Long weekend
62. Excuse me
63. You're confused
64. Midnight rendevous
65. Key ring
66. Copyright
67. Lean over backwards
68. Headquarters
69. Let bygones be bygones
70. Angle of incidence
71. I'm in love with you
72. Open season
73. One night stand
74. Money market
75. Head over heels in love

All Aboard ***

(The 1980's answer to the 1950's stunt of how many people can fit into a telephone booth.)

Object: to see how many people can get on the 2'x2' platform at one time.

Rules:

1. In order to be counted as on the platform, each person must have both feet off the ground.
2. The group must be able to hold a balanced pose for at least five seconds; i.e., no one touches the ground for 5 measured seconds.

106

Note: An average group can get 12-15 bodies on the platform, although theoretically a much larger number is possible. The exercise lends itself to useful discussion about team effort, group and individual commitment, leadership, compassion, and group problem-solving dynamics.

The All Aboard is a solidly built 2'x2' platform. The 2'x2' measurement is not carved in stone (in fact, each platform I build seems to vary a few inches from side to side), but does provide a general pattern size to work from. In addition, if you don't build a standard sized platform, how can you sponsor an NCAA-sanctioned All Aboard Championship?

Construction of a portable platform is simplicity itself. Cut two 2 ft. sections of 4"x4" lumber and, placing them parallel to one another 2 ft. apart,(outside edges), nail or screw three-2"x8"x2' boards to the top of the 4"x4"'s. Finish the job by rasping off the edges to minimize the chance of injury if someone were to fall onto the platform.

By fabricating a portable platform (rather than the old, sunk-in-the-ground model), you have the flexibility to present this activity where it best suits the weather or your needs. For variety, give a larger group (20-25) a 3' x 3' platform to serve as a landing area for the swinging All Aboard problem, also called Prouty's Landing.

Remember that one of your responsibilities as group leader is to encourage safety procedures. It may be necessary to occasionally nix an idea if someone's safety is jeopardized. The "Pig Pile" technique of stacking people on the platform in cordwood fashion is dangerous and should not be allowed. This seemingly logical ploy of stacking horizontal participants perpendicular to one another (think of a tic-tac-toe set-up) results in tremendous pressure being put on the bottom two people. Perform some quick addition and you will see what a poor solution this becomes—theoretically sound; actually, painful.

An initiative problem variation of an old playground favorite: the teeter totter (TT).

The object is to balance a small group (10-12) on top of the TT log for ten seconds. If the log touches the ground at either end, at any time, the event must start again; i.e., everyone off the log. Participants are allowed to climb on the log only at the long end (fulcrum to end). An easier variation includes starting over only if the log touches the ground at the far end.

A safety addition to prevent after-hours teeter totter SLAM-BANG, is to bury a "dead man" immediately below the long end of the TT log. A dead man is any heavy or large surface area device that is buried to act as an anchor for something. Attach a section of 5/16" cable to the dead man so that a seized (swaged or cabled clamped) end of the cable protrudes above the ground. Place a ½" nut eye bolt through the end of the TT log so that a lock can be attached through this eye bolt to the seized end of the dead man cable. This convenient anchor's quaint name (dead man) does little to engender feelings of trust, but there never has been much safety in syntax.

Building the TT log device itself is an easy matter. Dig two holes about 12" apart and 2-½' deep. Place two 5-½' long sections of telephone poles vertically into the holes, fill with dirt and tamp solidly. Ask a conveniently assembled group of lifters to hold the TT log horizontal to the ground between the two vertical poles and about 10" from their top. Drill through the posts and log with 5/8" extension auger bit. Use a power drill; the lifters will appreciate your thoughtfulness.

Then bang a 5/8" diameter bolt through the hole, and tighten on a nut. Use a washer at the end of the bolt. You may want to attach a cotter pin or peen over the edges of the bolt to prevent vandalism. Make sure during the drilling process that the teeter log is held so that the fulcrum point is somewhere around ⅓ the length of the log (not at its balance point: too easy). Rip the top of the TT log with a chain saw to provide good footing. A touch or two of the chain will do—don't start sculpting a totem pole.

Do not allow any student to be under either end of the log at any time.

This neat balance event can be easily extended by building another TT arrangement so that the second TT log is perpendicular to, and comes down near the end of, the first TT log. Then build another one perpendicular to that one and then...

107

Touch My Can *

Object: For a group of about 12-15 participants to make physical contact with an empty pop or beer can without making physical contact with one another. One person's proboscis must also be touching the can. Hair, more than 4 inches from the head, does not count as a point of contact. This is an announced get-to-know-you up close and personal initiative problem.

Big Business **

I like this problem's potential. It has all the right ingredients for an engrossing, useful, and enjoyable initiative task. There is one substantial drawback: the necessary building blocks (an integral part of the problem) are either fairly expensive or very expensive. But let's take a look at the makings of this entrepreneurial delight, before pulling out our pockets and summarily dismissing an insightful activity.

Your group (keep the numbers small: 4-5) is charged with construction of a free-standing tower of any shape or size using only the provided building materials.

The company you own won an invitation to build a small scale tower to prove that your architects and builders can do it for the least cost and the highest profit. Obviously other invited contractors will be clawing at the same mercenary gains.

There are two stages to this problem. These two stages are structured to allow enough time to complete the problem in a class period (45-50 minutes).

Stage One (20 minutes). Plan your tower (architects) and practice building a prototype or two (builders). You may take the blocks from the container and build as many practice towers as you like (lots of trial and error), but at the end of this stage all the blocks must be disengaged and placed back in the box.

Stage Two (16 minutes). From the START, your group must construct a free-standing tower (erect long enough to be measured by the judge). This building period is timed. After recording the final time, number of blocks, and the height of the tower, the three BIG BUSINESS GRAPHS are used to determine your result: the profit.

Clarifications and Real Life $

Hints. Allow 200 LEGO blocks (or a facsimile) per team. Include more small blocks than large ones. Also include a base plate to provide stability. If you don't know what LEGO is, ask any married friend with young children. I'm sure there are other building implements on the market that are usable for this problem and which don't cost as much as LEGO.

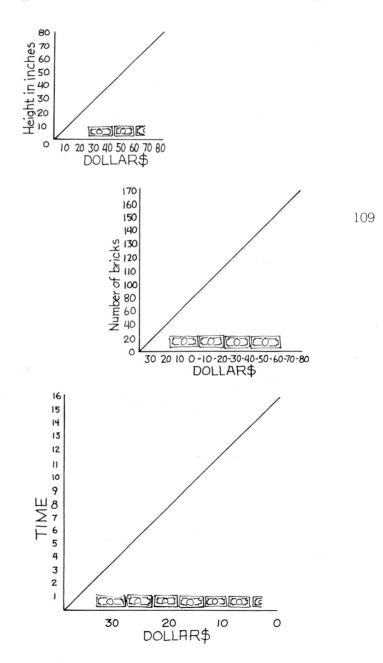

$BIG BUSINESS GRAPHS$

Can't drive a nail without whacking a digit or two? Get the hives when you look at a blueprint? Develop a headache when you read "...and then put Tab A into Slot B, when B has been folded under Slot C"? Here's balm for your shattered ego, a genuinely easy to build and use initiative problem called, "The TP Shuffle."

Materials List

One - 30 foot telephone pole

Tools Needed

None, Zero, Not any

Can't beat that can you? If you like the flow so far, you'll love the building directions.

Building Directions:

With a class or a few strong friends, place the chosen telephone pole (TP) horizontally on a flat grassy or ungrassy area. Done! Hoo Ha was that great? I could build ropes courses all day!

If you also are interested in what to do with that pole lying out there, here are the details, and it's even more fun than building it.

Ask a group of about twenty people to halve themselves, and with their newly formed group to stand (balance) on opposite ends of the TP so that the two groups are facing one another in single file. Establishing this face-to-face queue is not the problem. The essential difficulty lies in having the two groups exchange ends of the pole without touching the ground. Time the entire procedure and assign a 15 second time penalty for *every* touch with the turf (man and woman eating alfalfa sprouts). After a completed attempt, encourage the group to talk things over and give it another try; the sprouts are still hungry.

As with all these timed initiative problems, it is important to attempt the problem more than once. The first attempt establishes a time to beat. Additional attempts invariably result in a faster time as the result of cooperation, planning, individual effort, etc. Beating a PB (personal best) is the best kind of competition. Let it happen by allowing enough time for more than one effort.

Rule Refinements and Variations on the TP Shuffle

As the individuals exchange ends, they do not have to assume any particular sequence at the beginning or end of the task, just so that the groups have switched ends from N to S, or E to W, or NE to SW, or SSE to NNW, or...

If you have just purchased a new set of tools and feel chagrined that you are not going to get a chance to smash your thumb, here's a variation that requires some building.

Dig two holes with a post hole digger (PHD) about 18 feet apart and 2 feet deep. Cut two 3 foot sections of pole, place them in the holes and tamp in dirt firmly around them. *Do not* cut these 3 foot sections from your 30 footer.

Lift the long pole and rest it horizontally on top of the two short poles; the longer pole then being parallel to and about twelve inches off the ground. Drill the top pole at each end with a 5/8 inch extension auger bit so that the drilled holes extend well into the two vertical short poles. With a sledge hammer, drive 5/8"x18" machine bolts through these holes and into the lower support poles so that the bolt heads are flush with the pole. These bolts might be obtained, with a bit of luck and cajoling, from an electric or telephone company. If you can't scrounge or buy bolts, perhaps a sheet metal strap placed over the top pole and bolted to the vertical poles beneath, might do the trick. A drop of "Crazy Glue," notwithstanding the manfacturer's impressive advertisements, will not suffice.

The people problem is the same, but the twelve inch elevation of the log allows a bit more maneuverability for the participants and facilitates penalty spotting by the instructor. The elevated pole also proves easier to move on because there is no roll to the pole (like that?), but high or low, it's an enjoyable problem.

111

Group Juggling **

This simplistic, by-the-numbers, macro-motor activity has been around for years because it's easy to teach and fun to accomplish.

Ask your large group to break up into smaller groups of 5-7. Meanwhile, have available enough comparatively soft, throwable objects (nerf balls, softies, bean bags, tennis balls), so that there are a few more than one per person.

Have the group stand in a circle facing one another, and so that the circle's diameter is no more than 12-15 feet.

One person in a group of 6 keeps the throwable objects nearby and lobs one of them to a person across the circle. That person lobs the ball to a person opposite from him/her and this continues until a person-to-person sequence is set. Do not throw to the person next to you.

Once everybody knows whom to throw to and receive from, the initiator starts the ball again, but this time includes another ball and eventually another until there are six balls being kept aloft simultaneously. Try reversing the sequence; i.e., throwing to the person you formerly received from.

Try keeping seven objects going with only six people throwing—now *that's* juggling!

Ship Wreck *

A peripatetic "all aboard" problem. The object of Ship Wreck is to gain the most points during the activity through group cooperation and fast action!

Materials:

large field
½" plywood circles 3 or 4 feet in diameter for each group to use as a "ship." Rasp and sand the sharp edges and splinters from each side of the plywood.

Procedure:

1. Divide participants into two groups with 8-10 members per group.
2. Give each group a "ship" and instruct all members to hold onto its sides as they run the length of a playing field.
3. Groups are to run with their "ship" until a staff member yells "Shark!" Then, all members jump on board the "ship." The first group with *all feet* off the ground, gains a point. Repeat this procedure several times. The first group to reach the finish line gains 3 points.
4. Add up points to decide the winner, or forget the points and play "go fish" to decide the winner.
5. Debrief with specific suggestions on how to improve next time.
6. Repeat the activity if the group had fun the first time.

For younger or larger groups, use hula hoops in place of the plywood sections.

Human Ladder **

Note: The direction of the ladder may change at any time (e.g., right angle turn). Obstacles may be added and the height of the rungs also may vary.

Discussion: How did you feel when you were climbing? When you were holding the rung? Did your feelings change after the first climber passed by your position? Did trusting some people make your climb easier? Do not allow rung holders to position the rungs higher than their shoulders.

Purpose: To develop trust, to be responsible for each other's safety, to engage in unself-conscious physical contact with members of your group.

Materials: 6-10 smooth hardwood dowel rods about 3 feet long, 1¼" in diameter.

Directions: Participants are paired and given one "rung" of the ladder. Several pairs, holding a rung and standing close together, form the ladder. A climber starts at one end of the ladder and proceeds to move from one rung to another. As the climber passes by, the pair holding that ladder rung may leave their position and proceed to the end of the ladder, extending the ladder length indefinitely.

This initiative problem is becoming more popular and rightly so; it's inexpensive, fits almost anywhere, can be made portable, and has the right mix of challenge and fantasy.

The object is to move your entire group through a nylon fabricated web without touching the web material (nylon cord). Four or five small bells can be tied anywhere on the web so that movement of the cords (a touch) is transferred to the bell(s). A sounding of a bell indicates that the participant has been felt by the spider and he/she must begin again to keep from being eaten, or wrapped in silken cords to be eaten later. Try to find one of those horrible looking rubber spiders at the five and dime and dangle it threateningly from one of the nylon threads—a touch of the bizzare to add fantasy and fun.

To make the event more challenging, the rule exists that <u>a body can pass through a web opening only once.</u> This obviously adds to the group commitment and the necessity of working together. Number your group so that there are at least as many web openings as there are bodies to pass through. Everytime I fabricate a web, I seem to learn something that makes the next one easier to build.

Some tips:

1) Use nylon cord. The stretch characteristic of this tying material allows the web to remain taut (under tension). Parachute cord seems to work best—strong, elastic and with a "web-like" diameter.

2) Place 6 anchor points in the two vertical support posts or trees. These anchors can be any type of substantial eyescrew. I've recently started using a large (3/8"x5") galvanized staple as a non-critical (no belay) connector for ropes course work. You just hammer them in and, considering their simplicity, the holding power is impressive. The anchor points are placed at about 7', 4' and 1'.

3) Tie one end of the nylon cord to any one of the anchor points and begin reeving the free end through the other anchors in sequence, to make a rectangular outline with the cord. While doing this, take a turn around each anchor and pull the

cord tight (play-a-tune-on-it tight). Read #4 before proceeding.

4) If you didn't read this and have been enthusiastically cutting and stringing cord—STOP—I have back-up instructions. The loops (figure 8 or butterfly knots) must be tied while stringing the cord to ensure proper placement of the loops (symmetry, as any Tom Noddy knows). The loops serve as anchor points for the "web" strands, and allow practically an unlimited variety of web patterns.

5) Using the loops and anchors, tie up a unique web arrangement, remembering that people of all sizes must be able to fit through the web gaps. If you haven't tried this initiative problem before, I think you will be surprised at how small an opening a person can get through (with help).

Safety Consideration and Ponderable Possibilities:

a. Do not allow people to dive through the web. There is the distinct possibility of neck injury, cord burn and web destruction.

b. Allow participants to go under the web, but not over.

c. Try to fabricate a web that will allow a put-up/take-down function; perhaps using short Bunji (shock) cords at the anchor points. I haven't tried this yet—it's just an idea. Be fair—let me know the results.

Try using waxed nylon cord for the actual web strands. It's thinner than the periphery parachute cord and has a more web-like look. The waxed cord also holds a knot well.

114

The Clock **

It would be almost impossible to convince a sophisticated coed group of high school students that playing a merry-go-round game can be fun and challenging. However, asking a group to see how quickly they can complete the "clock" requirement accomplishes just that.

After having completed a few warm-up exercises, ask the group to form a large hand-in-hand circle.

Indicate to the circled group that you would like them to rotate clockwise 360° in one direction and then return 360° back to the start. The goal is to see how quickly the group can complete the double rotation. The attempt is timed and time is stopped if anyone breaks his/her grip with a partner. Group cooperation is obviously essential. A good time for 30-35 people is anything below 30 seconds. In establishing a time goal, assign about one second per player, subtracting an additional second for every ten participants.

Place sweatshirts (or some such markers) at both "six o'clock" and "twelve o'clock" (3 and 9 o'clock too, if you're compulsive) inside the circle, so that the group has boundaries to rotate around and reference points for starting and finishing.

If you want to increase the difficulty of this moving problem, ask the group to begin in a seated-on-the-ground position and also finish up in that position. The clock stops when the last person sits on the ground.

If the group breaks contact three separate times, stop the activity for that day and suggest coming back to it at another time. It gives the group something to look forward to and encourages after-class conversation.

In your debriefing discussion, ask these questions to encourage group interaction:

1. Why did the group have so much trouble retaining a connected grip?

2. What could have been done to keep the group together as they attempted the double rotation?

3. Is it important to have fast people in the group?

4. Would it have been more efficient to exclude the slow runners? More satisfying?

This activity is an example of how a well known child's pastime (ring-around-the-rosie) can be adapted and embellished to produce a challenging initiative problem.

Knots (Tangle, Hands) ***

This no-prop people problem has been around for a long time and rightly so; it's easy to set up and often sparks cooperation from balky or bored groups.

Ask a group of 10-16 individuals to face one another in a tight circle. Each person holds out their right hand and grasps the right hand of someone else, as if they were shaking hands. Then each person extends their left hand and grasps the hand of someone else, so that each person is holding two different hands. This hand-in-hand configuration should come out equal. With hands tightly held, arms intertwined and bodies juxtaposed, it's time to explain the problem.

The Gordian group is to try and unwind themselves from their tangled situation so that after much try-this, try-that squirming and contorting, a hand-in-hand circle is formed. The physical hand-to-hand contact that you have with your partner cannot be broken in order to facilitate an unwinding movement. Sweaty palms may pivot on one another, but skin contact may not be lost. As a result of the initial grasping movements, and depending upon the number of participants, two or even three distinct people circles may form. These circles are sometimes intertwined like Ballantine rings. Sometimes the people in the final circle(s) will alternate facing directions and that's OK—be lenient, this problem already has enough difficulty built in.

If the group has been struggling with a "knot" for longer than your session has time, offer an honorable out called *Knot First Aid.* Indicate that actual hands and arms knots do sometimes materialize in this jumble of anatomical parts and that it may become necessary to effect a cure by deciding, amongst the group, which grip needs knot first aid; i.e., which pair of hands should separate and regrip. Solutions are often quickly achieved after this bit of help, but I have seen knots that needed 2nd aid! Don't be too quick to offer an easy out if time and inclination seem to indicate a continued struggle. Some groups "get into" this problem and will express their desire to continue.

118

PLYNN

Rabid Nugget Rescue *

Use as a lead-up to Blindfold Soccer; helps develop trust and cooperation.

Partner throws a "rabid nugget" (tennis ball) as far as possible and then verbally (no physical contact) guides his/her blindfolded partner to the ball. Once retrieved, the ball is brought back and placed in a rabid nugget hospital (box). Task complete. Switch roles.

This exercise is particularly intense if a lot of trees or ground dips are part of the search route.

The object of this initiative problem is to move your entire group (usually 10-12) from a safe area over a designated poisoned-peanut butter plot to the far safe side using only the provided props. A grassy area works best for safety and aesthetics, but a gym floor or parking lot are also usable.

If anyone touches the taboo area while trying to cross over, assign a time penalty of 15 seconds per touch. Such a minor penalty keeps the participants honest, but also allows continued movement and momentum. Returning to the starting line because of each flub might result in an overnight camping situation.

Trolley Construction and Use

Trolley 4"x4"'s can be as short or long as your group needs dictate. A trolley two feet long with room for only two people is useful for a special needs population or for younger students that have trouble cooperating beyond a one-on-one situation. Trolleys up to 16' long have been built for large groups.

Buy the least expensive 4"x4" stock available. Even rough cut green wood is OK for this event. Don't try fabricating the trolleys from 2"x4" stock because the 2" measurement (which is actually 1½") isn't deep enough to countersink the knots. If you leave the knots on the surface of the boards it makes the "walking" attempts frustratingly difficult.

Using a try-square, draw a line across the 4"x4" board every 12", and on this line, find the center of the board. Using a 1½" drill bit, drill each one of these center marks to a depth of 2". A spade bit (speed-bor) does a good job of making these holes (set up a drill powerful enough to handle such a large-headed bit). These holes also can be drilled using a bit brace and an Irwin adjustable bit. I mention this only because I have drilled a few boards this way (years ago) and know that it can be accomplished. If your boards measure 12" long, that means you have 20 holes to drill; a substantial physical commitment for one person. If you have students helping, a bit brace can be more meaningful from an I-helped-build-it standpoint.

Using a ¾″ bit, drill through each large countersunk hole on center. (To keep the drill bit from splintering through the far side of the board, watch for the tip of the spade bit to just break the surface; then turn the 4″x4″ over and, using this pinhole as a guide, drill in the reverse direction.)

Cut 20 five-foot long pieces of half inch polypropalene rope. I choose poly rope because of its strength, bright color, and its comparative inexpensiveness. Reeve a cut section of rope through each hole. (It may be necessary to tape an end of the rope to make it fit through the ¾″ hole without fraying.) Tie an overhand knot in the rope end existing from the large countersunk hole. Tighten the knot as close to the end of the rope as possible without dissolving the knot. Pull the knot into the countersunk hole with a jerk on the other end of the rope. Any part of the knot which sticks above the plane of the board must be tapped into the hole with a hammer. Using a propane torch, burn each inserted knot sufficiently so that it partially melts in the hole and cannot be untied accidentally.

Either tie another overhand knot in the opposite end of the rope, or if you have the time and patience, perform a back splice in each rope end. This end knot or splice provides the students with a handle.

Using a medium rasp, remove all sharp corners and splinters from the board.

Implementation and Variations

If you want to make the event a bit more difficult, drill the first and last hole only 2 inches in from the end of the 4″x4″. This provides rope for two additional people, but less board feet to stand on.

When you ask the group to use these props to move from point A to point B, don't set the 4″x4″'s on the ground parallel to the destination. Throw them down or cross them so that their relative position to one another doesn't indicate possible usage.

Tie another overhand knot about ⅓ of the way down each rope. After the group has mastered the 1-2-3 right, 1-2-3 left technique movement, suggest that they try making forward progress by all holding onto the lower knots. This bentover "spoon" position makes the group more vulnerable to the domino phenomena.

If you have a hot-shot, I-can-do-anything leader type who needs a bit of humbling, suggest that he/she take the first position on the boards and call signals from there.

A section of undrilled 4″x4″ can be included on the field as an obstacle that must be crossed as part of the problem. The results of this attempted crossing are usually humorous. Don't point out the efficient side-step technique of crossing the 4″x4″ obstacle until the problem is being debriefed.

A video tape of the problem-solving process, particularly with this event, is a valuable and entertaining teaching tool.

The following rejuvenated group initiative problem, called the *Playpen,* fell into disfavor many years ago because of an unfortunate accident (broken sternum) that was the result of an after hours slip. The *Playpen,* nevertheless, is a useful group problem that indicates the value of efficiently working together and is functionally safe if unauthorized use can be avoided.

Get out your PHD (post hole digger) and get set for a strenuous upper body workout. Dig a series of 2½' deep holes arranged in a circle that measures about 40' in circumference. There should be 15 holes placed about 2' apart.

Cut a series of trunks and limbs of various lengths, (from 4' - 6') and of a minimum 4″ in diameter. Some of these stumps can be left bifurcated to provide a unique stance.

To retard rot, pour some creosote into the bottom of the holes before placing the stumps. Use black locust wood if available and forget about rot.

Set the posts as vertically as possible and tamp the dirt fill with gusto. There you go...now you have a *Playpen.*

Ask a group of 15 students to stand in a circle behind the stumps of the Playpen. On a signal (GO works fairly well) they are to mount the stumps (one student per stump) and join hands. This simple group erection is timed from GO to hand joining. Ask the group to try again to see if they can better their initial time, (probably a minute or so). With a bit of thought and cooperation their time should drop dramatically and continue to decrease for their 3rd and 4th attempts. The emphasis, of course, is on group efficiency in contrast to individual stumbling about—it works and the results are undeniable. *Do not* allow anyone to step from stump top to stump top in an attempt to "walk" around the Playpen: sternums have been known to suffer.

Traffic Jam **

I forget the correct moves to this problem almost every time I present it, but I have yet to see a group that didn't eventually come up with a solution. So don't worry about remembering the answer, just get the rules straight and then look sagely amused by their attempts, offering an occasional "Hmmmmmm" or "What do you think?" to solidify your all-knowing aura.

The object of this largely cerebral problem is to have two groups of people exchange places on a line of squares that has one more place than the number of people in both groups.

The physical set-up can be arranged almost anywhere. The boxes, indicated in the illustration, can be marked with chalk, masking tape, scratched in the dirt or be paper plates, scrap paper, etc. The marks or markers should be placed an easy step from one another.

Rules:

To begin, one group stands on the places to the left of the middle square, the other group stands to the right. Both groups face the middle unoccupied square.

Using the following moves, people on the left side must end up in the places on the right side, and vice versa.

Illegal Moves:

1. Any move backwards.
2. Any move around someone facing the same way you are; i.e., you are looking at their back.
3. Any move which involves two persons moving at once.

Legal Moves:

1. A person may move into an empty space in front of him/her.
2. A person may move around a person who is facing him into an empty space. Thus,

a.

Here, 1 or 2 may move into the empty space.

b.

Here, 1 may move into the empty space, because two people are facing one another.

Note: This is often a difficult problem. Thus, it is not recommended for younger children.

After a solution to the problem is discovered (or chanced upon) and the group discovers that one person giving commands is the most efficient way to solve the "traffic jam," ask that individual and the group if they can quickly solve the problem again. The leader will ordinarily stumble a bit in a repeat attempt, but the solution will eventually be reached more efficiently.

Ask the group to try it once again, indicating that you have an additional challenge for them and that successful completion of this addition depends upon complete understanding of the solution.

When they appear confident with their solution, have them line up on the squares in a "start" position. Indicate that completion of this next challenge involves having everyone go through the solution moves of the original problem while *holding their breath*. The leader, who stands apart from the group, is the only one allowed to give commands, and breathe. If anyone breathes before the last move, the whole group expires in horrible agony (but not before bludgeoning their fumbling leader) and must begin again!

This is one of the few problems in which a group will eventually decide to have one person take charge and for the others to be quiet and follow directions. This is worth talking about in comparison to other initiative tests, and other life situations. It can lead to a useful discussion of leadership styles, the selection process of the leader, the experience of being a follower, etc.

Two by Four (2x4) **

This is a tabletop problem usually attempted with black and red checkers. In this case, substitute people for checkers and male and female for colors. It's a semi-cerebral problem that usually requires more trial and error than thinking.

Ask 8 people to line up shoulder-to-shoulder facing you, alternating male/female. See if the group can end up with males on one side of the line and females on the other, utilizing the following rules and guidelines:

1. The criterion is to complete the problem in the least number of moves. Four moves is the minimum. Don't announce the minimum until an initial try has been made.
2. All moves must be made as pairs. Anyone next to you is a potential member of a pair; male or female.
3. As a pair moves, they leave an empty slot in the line which must remain and be eventually filled by another pair.
4. Pairs may not pivot or turn around.
5. The final line must be solid; i.e., no gaps.

The following number sequences illustrate the 4-move solution:

If the group is suffering from terminal frustration, give them the first correct move. Such largesse increases the group's belief that the solution is imminent and depending upon their outlook, that's either one less more than 4, or 3, to go.

If you forget the solution or neglect to reproduce the above solution on your palm, don't panic, just appear slightly amused at their attempts or sagely tolerant coupled with an occasional smile or slight affirmative nod of the head until the students eventually hit on the right combination. If 2 or 3 hours have gone by and your nod is more weary than reinforcing you may have to postpone the solution (escape route #7) by suggesting that they "sleep on it."

123

♂ ♀ ♂ ♀ ♂ ♀ ♂ ♀ ①
1 (2 3) 4 5 6 7 8

♂   ♀ ♂ ♀ ♂ ♀ ♀ ♂
1 ② 4 (5 6) 7 8 2 3

♂ ♂ ♀ ♀   ♂ ♀ ♀ ♂
1 5 6 4 ③ 7 (8 2) 3

♂ ♂ ♀ ♀ ♀ ♀ ♂   ♂
(1 5) 6 4 8 2 7 ④   3

♀ ♀ ♀ ♀ ♂ ♂ ♂ ♂
6 4 8 2 7 1 5 3

Zig Zag **

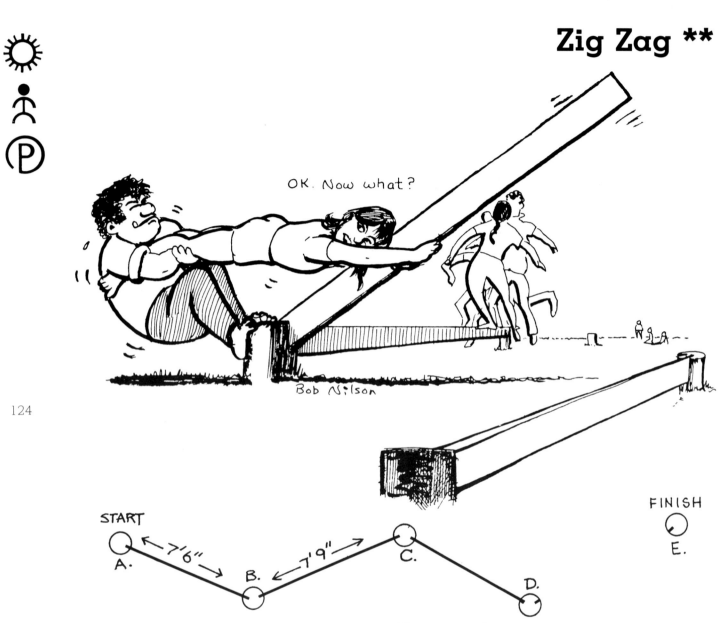

OK. Now what?

Bob Nilson

START

A. ←— 7'6" —→ B. ←— 7'9" —→ C.

D.

FINISH
E.

Object:

To transport a group across a designated area without touching the ground with either the available boards or any part of a participant's body.

Rules:

1. For the boards to be used, they must fit into the slotted posts; i.e., they may not be turned flat and placed on top of a post.
2. If a participant's body or a board touches the ground, a time penalty may be assigned or the group may be required to start over.

Construction:

1. 2"x6's should be used as crossing boards.
2. Board BC should be equal to the space DE.
3. Board AB and CD should be less than the distance between DE so that only board BC will fit space DE.
4. Posts are placed so that approximately 14 inches of the post is above ground and 3 feet is in the ground. The top of the posts are notched appropriately for the boards with a chain saw or chisel.
5. Distances AB and CD measure 7 feet 6 inches, and distance BC measures 7 feet 9 inches.

Punctured Drum *

Object:

Given a multi-punctured 55 gallon drum, two one gallon pots (or similar containers), and a fast-flowing or easily attainable source of water, the group must attempt to fill the drum to overflowing.

Rules:

Only portions of the participants' anatomies may be used to plug the holes.

Considerations:

The number of holes must necessarily vary with the size of the group. Puncture 120 holes (16p nail size) in the drum (which duplicates the number of fingers in a group of 12). Think of the anatomical problems that result from widely spaced holes and proceed drilling compassionately. You may temporarily plug some holes (cut sections of dowel or cork) when the drum is to be used by a smaller group. How far you place the drum from the water source varies the degree of difficulty.

Simon Mendez

Bridge It **

Here's a six-person problem that requires a unique solution.

The object is to move the A-Frame apparatus and one person aboard, from point A to point B (30 ft.), using the five available 18' sling ropes. This problem works well on grass or asphalt. I haven't tried it on ice, but it sounds ludicrous enough for an attempt.

Rules:

1. The A-Frame must maintain at least one point of contact with the ground at all times and never more than two points of contact.
2. Only one person can make body contact with the A-Frame apparatus and he/she must avoid contact with the ground.
3. The ropes may not touch the ground at any time during the passage over the restricted (taboo) area.
4. All the helpers can be no closer than 5' to the A-Frame during movement of the frame. Tie a knot in the rope at 5' to help the folks maintain this distance.

A Solution:

Tie the five sling ropes to the apex of the A-Frame using a series of bowlines, clove hitches or whatever knot(s) you feel comfortable with. Stand the frame vertically (2 points of contact at the base) and ask one of the six participants to stand on the horizontal cross bar. As this individual rocks from side to side (each left/right rocking motion is coupled with a thrust forward), the other five participants support the A-Frame with the previously attached sling ropes. There is scant chance of the frame and rider falling over if the rope holders remain alert.

The A-Frame itself can be built from lashed saplings, or more uniformly from sections of 2"x3" lumber bolted together with three 3/8" x 3½" carriage bolts.

I'm sure you have been to conferences or clinics where they "teach" communications procedures, team building, pyramidal management, organizational and developmental skills—need I impress you any further? What it comes down to is this: are you learning anything about the jargon-loaded skills mentioned above, or are you being burdened with a series of valid but inappropriate (and perhaps boring) techniques for whatever "people" skills are being touted?

Recently, I was introduced to a "people" skills teaching game that sparked total enthusiasm, resulted in an engrossing task and was (hallelujah) fun.

Split your group (16-20) in half. The method employed for this halving is worth repeating also. Rip two full page pictures out of a magazine and cut them into jigsaw-like pieces to equal the number of people in the group (so that the pieces from both pictures equal the total number of people). Toss all the pieces willy-nilly into a container and ask each participant to draw out one piece. After all the pieces have been drawn, ask the players to pool their pieces to make a picture—two defined pictures—cigarette or Kotex ads are probably not appropriate. You get the picture.

You will need the following props x 2; i.e., one set for each group:
- 4 - styrofoam cups
- 8 - 8" small diameter sticks (to be gathered previously by the participants).
- 1 - roll of masking tape
- 1 - small box of LEGO or Tinker Toys or the like
- 1 - paper & pencil (or pen)
- 1 - set of terminology

You will also need the following items to be used by both groups:
- 2 - card tables
- 1 - sheet or blanket
- 1 - chair for each person
- 2 - rooms

Set-Up Procedure:

Place the card tables next to one another. Hang the sheet or blanket vertically over the separation point of the tables. (How you suspend the sheet is your pre-initiative problem.) Divide the chairs equally on each side of the sheet.

Place all props for each group on separate tables.

The terminology change papers should read something like this: Side A—The word *top* means *bottom; side* means *under*; and a *laugh* means *high.*

Side B—The word *tape* means *wide*; sticking out your tongue means *how many*; and *criss-cross* means *parallel.*

Procedure: Explain to both groups that the tangible purpose of this exercise is for each separate group to build a bridge toward the other group (sheet) so that *the bridges meet and look as much alike as possible.* Do not offer any guidelines except to say that only the offered props may be used. Try fabricating a story about two countries that are separated by a body of water but want to establish a trade and cultural relationship. The river is plagued by bad weather and almost constant fog. The countries have a common language but the dialects differ considerably. In order to establish a necessary dialogue between groups, three five minute meetings have been arranged (be very strict on the timing) at a common meeting site (another room). As the members adjourn to the meeting room, remind them that they must not look on the other side of the sheet; offer blindfolds if necessary.

Only one member from each group may talk at each meeting, and these two individuals sit facing one another, separate from the other people in the room. No comments from the group are allowed during this time (only laughter!).

The timing of the planning and building sessions should look like this: Separate groups are shown their building area and props and are given seven minutes to talk over the problems of building the bridge (amongst themselves, *not* with the other group) and to begin construction

if they choose to.

1st: 5 minute meeting of the chosen group representative in a separate room. A new representative should be chosen each time. 7 minute discussion and building time back at the site.

2nd: 5 minute representative meeting 5 minute discussion and building time

3rd: (final) 5 minute representative meeting 10 minute race to get the work accomplished.

Be strict as to the deadline. Then comes the unveiling (and groans of dismay or shouts of glee) and a period of time set aside for debriefing the process, levels of accomplishment, and comparison of approach.

The physical result is apt to surprise you by the architectural accuracy achieved.

The problem and process is engrossing, revealing, and fun.

128

Macro Tangrams *

You have probably tried to solve puzzles like these (see illustrations) at one time or another, but on a smaller physical scale. A group solution of the puzzle necessitates some sense of spatial relationship and an appreciation of leader/follower roles to efficiently discover the figure forming positions for the jigsaw-like pieces.

The ----------- marks are erasure lines and are there only to indicate the easiest way to locate the cut lines.

Cut the puzzle pieces from ½ inch fiber board (an inexpensive and fairly tough plywood substitute) or whatever durable materials you have available. The sections are cut much larger than the commercially packaged pieces, in order to facilitate group interaction.

Hand out the unassembled pieces to the first problem (use small groups of 3-5 people) and ask the enigma experts to form a Greek Cross Red Cross symbol). After they have accomplished this task, ask them to form a square using the same pieces.

The other three puzzles should be self-explanatory as to what shapes or configurations form the solution.

Use the measured distances as proportion guides only. If you want the figures bigger or smaller, keep the proportions the same and cut away.

After the group has solved the problems, or occasionally not come up with a solution, ask a question or two about how the group interacted (or ignored one another) to stimulate conversation about something other than rock music, video games, the Celtics, or blemishes. Here's an effective way to allow a person to express him/herself.

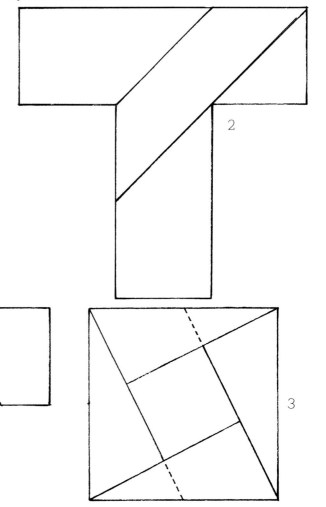

1

2

3

An interesting exercise in communication skills results from asking two people to sit back-to-back on the floor and then supplying one of the individuals with an assembled tangram puzzle. The other participant sits looking at the jumbled pieces of an identical puzzle. The person with the assembled puzzle attempts to verbally explain to his/her mute partner how to put the pieces together to achieve congruent solutions.

The procedure and eventual solution can be turtle-like or impressively swift. A joint working knowledge of geometric vocabulary makes the task much easier.

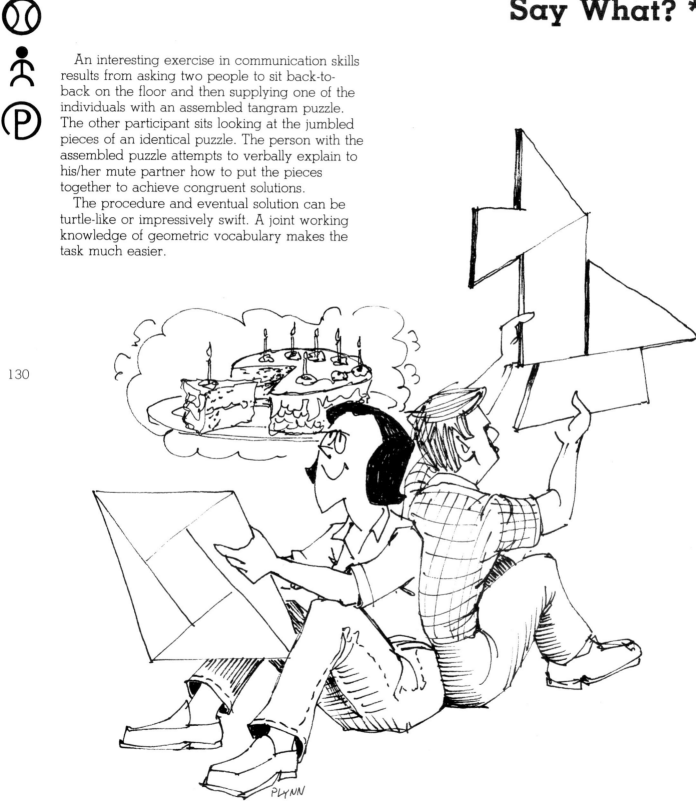

PLYNN

The Almost Infinite Circle **

This rope play is a time-honored party game that seems to offer no solution (particularly after the first hour of bondage).

Object:

To separate two loosely connected individuals from a seemingly impossible, but engagingly simple, intertwinement of ropes. Refer to the illustration to help visualize the physical set-up.

Procedure:

Tie each end of the 10' long rope comfortably around the wrists. How tightly (painfully) the wrist loops are drawn has nothing to do with the problem. Uncomfortably tight ropes should be avoided.

Allow as much time as necessary for the solution to be discovered. Once the solution is discovered, it will soon become common knowledge.

Rules:

Two intertwined people must separate from one another without (1) cutting the rope; (2) untying the knots; or (3) slipping the knotted portion over their hands.

Answer as many non-solution questions as the entwined pair ask and continually emphasize that there is a solution, because logic indicates that a sharp knife is the only answer.

Solution:

1. Take a bight in the center of your partner's rope.
2. Pass this bight under either of your wrist loops so that the bight portion is closest to your fingers.
3. Pull the bight through with your other hand and open it to a size that will accommodate your hand.
4. Pass the bight over your hand and
5. Pull it down and through the wrist loop.
6. You're free! You're not? Then let go of the rope with your teeth, check a dictionary to determine what a bight is and try again.

131

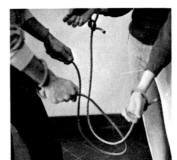
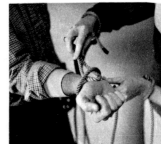

The Four Pointer or

The Monster **

This initiative problem is particularly useful for later discussion because the first technique chosen for a solution (see photograph) is usually the most difficult. Once a group "sees" the possibility of a solution, the blinders go on and they will collectively stick with that idea no matter how much sense it doesn't make.

The object is to get a group of seven people across a thirty-foot area, using only four anatomical points of *simultaneous* contact with the ground. A point of contact may be a foot, hand, knee, etc., but there can only be four parts of the group's anatomy on the floor at one time. The four points can be repeated over and over.

Rules:

1. All seven people must begin at the marked starting line and end at the finish line. Use the painted lines on a basketball court for convenience.
2. No props may be used (paper cores, wagons, mats).
3. All seven participants must be in constant and direct physical contact with each other as they make the crossing.

Considerations:

Divide a large group into many groups of 7. Explain the problem and then let the groups begin when ready so that the action is not seen as competitive. Obviously, groups will be looking at one another and perhaps hurrying their own efforts if they see another group having success, but a mass start dramatically increases the chance of injury. Also the results are not as much fun or as valuable for the participants if they feel rushed.

This problem can also be accomplished with other points of contact combinations. For example, five people and three points of contact.

133

Jelly Roll **

This is another initiative problem of the get-a-group-from-A-to-B-safely type. The object in this case is to transport an entire group over an area smeared with a poisonous jelly substance using only the following props:

1. Four jelly-resistant paper cores (large, durable, and surprisingly strong cardboard tubes). These cores, which can be obtained inexpensively (usually free) from industrial paper manufacturers, provide the basis for a number of initiative games and problems. The cores measure about 24 inches long by 12 inches in diameter. If you are having trouble locating these handy props, substitute smooth sided log sections of about the same dimensions. It's certainly more work to fashion the logs, but they will last a lot longer.

2. A stout pole measuring about 8 feet long and a 30 foot rope. Both of these items are resistant to the jelly.

3. A 2" x 10" x 12' board. This board should be relatively free of knots and unwarped. Rasp and sand the edges and corners of the board for safety reasons. The board is not resistant to the jelly.

The Actual Problem

Move your entire group from the near safe area to the far safe side over a 20-25 foot (depending upon the group's adeptness and ability to handle frustration) barrier of some noxious substance, the touching of which has dire consequences. Remember, in all these fabricated initiative-type problems, physical success is measured by getting the whole group through the task, not just the most capable members.

Rules:

1. The cores are jelly-resistant and may be freely rolled about in this viscous primordial ooze.
2. The board will dissolve if any part of it touches the jelly and the group either loses this prop or suffers some other unsavory consequence, (your choice).
3. Two short lengths of rope delineate the area to be crossed.
4. The jelly substance extends indefinitely in a lateral direction within the measured area; i.e., no one is going to walk around this obstacle.
5. If a participant touches (even slightly; this stuff is devastating) the jelly, she/he must quickly return to the starting point and copiously smear the jelly cleaning substance over their contaminated anatomy in order to begin afresh.
6. Walking purposefully into the jelly in order to advance the group's effort is not allowed and obviously unhealthy.
7. Instructors, because of their specially imported jelly-resistant shoes (made in Taiwan), may cavort freely within the confines of whatever nasty substance your imagination placed there.

Consideration

Do not set up this problem on a smooth gym floor. The paper cores will move too quickly and someone will eventually take a punishing fall. A wrestling mat or gymnastic floor exercise mat is okay for an attempt, but depends upon how the coaches feel about the use of their expensive pads.

135

PLYNN

The Electric Fence ***

Object:

To transport a group over an "electrified" wire or fence using only themselves and a conductive beam.

Rules:

1. If a participant touches the fence (rope), he is "zapped" and must attempt the crossing again. Any person touching the hapless victim as he/she touches the wire must also return for another crossing.
2. If the conductive beam (a small diameter log) touches the wire, all those in contact with that beam are "zapped" and must attempt another crossing.
3. An "electric force field" extends from the wire to the ground and cannot be penetrated.
4. The trees or other supports which hold up the "wire" are ironwoods (an excellent conductor) and cannot be safely touched.

Cautions:

a. Be careful not to let the more enthusiastic people literally throw other participants 7'-8' in the air over the ropes. Injury *will* soon result.
b. Do not let the last person perform a head-first dive into a shoulder roll. Trust dives, using spotters are OK even though such a dive seldom works and predictably zaps many catchers.
c. Encourage spotting.

Construction:

A. The "Electric Wire" can be a length of nylon slash rope or any substantial rope tied off in a triangular configuration to three support trees or poles. The electric fence problem can be accomplished with a single rope, between two trees, but I've found that a triangular set up is more visually challenging and safer. Safer because participants cannot get a running start in order to jump over the rope, and thus are less apt to take a chance.

B. A sturdy 8' pole, log, or 2"x4".

Note: Cut all the limbs or limb stumps from the 8' log to prevent injury. Dig up any and all protruding roots or rocks from the ground near the rope to prevent injury.

Vary the height of the rope as to the skill or age level of the group with whom you are working. 5' should be considered a maximum height.

136

PLYNN

The Amazon **

Object:

Using a plank, pole, a length of rope, and stick, the group must retrieve a container placed some distance from a simulated river bank.

Rules:

1. The participants may use only the given props and themselves.
2. If a participant touches the ground (water) between the bank and the container, he/she must go back to the bank and begin again.
3. Time penalties may be assigned every time the plank, stick, or individual touches the ground.

Construction:

A. 5/8" diameter multiline rope or slash goldline.
B. This pole should be at least 1½ inches in diameter. The pole does not have to be perfectly straight; a tree limb will suffice.
C. This plank should be at least six inches wide, two inches thick and preferably of hardwood.
D. The reaching pole may be constructed of any available material.
E. The container can be a #10 can with a wire handle attached.

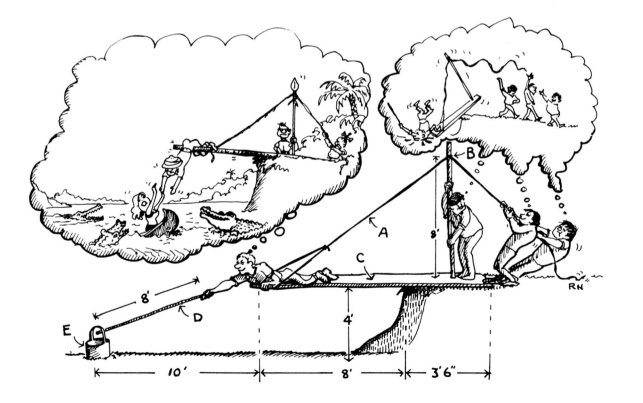

The Diminishing Load Problem **

Object:

To move a group or series of groups (teams) across an open field as quickly as possible. The distance can vary with the estimated strength of the groups. The width of a football field is a very physical distance.

Rules:

1. To cross the open area a person must be carried.
2. The carrier must return and be carried himself.
3. The only person allowed to walk (run) across the open area is the last person.
4. If the carried person touches the ground while being transported, both members must return to the start.
5. The number of people being carried and carrying can vary with the strength and/or imagination of the group; i.e., one-to-one is not the only way.

Variations:

The object can be to move the entire group across the distance in as few trips as possible (this changes the emphasis from speed to efficiency).

To include more of a trust factor, require that everyone wear blindfolds. Have at least 3 people available to act as spotters.

138

Nitro Crossing ***

Object:

To transport a group and a container, (#10 tin can) 7/8 full of "nitro" (water) across an open area using a swing rope.

Rules:

1. Participants must swing over a "trip wire" at the beginning and end of an open area without knocking either obstacle off its support. If a trip wire is knocked off, the entire group must go back and start again.
2. No knots may be tied in the swing rope; however, a bight may be taken. Tie a large knot in the bottom of the rope if help is needed for less adept students. This knot can be held tightly between the legs to help support the student's weight.
3. The "nitro" must be transported in such a way that NO water is spilled. If any spillage takes place (one drop), the entire group must start over. The container must be topped off at the 7/8 full mark after each spilling.
4. The swing rope must be obtained initially without stepping in the open area between the two trip wires.
5. The participants are allowed to use only themselves and their clothing to gain the swing rope.
6. Participants are not allowed to touch the ground while swinging between trip wires and must attempt the crossing again if they do so.

Variation:

The nitro problem can be accomplished indoors by utilizing a gymnasium climbing rope as the swing rope. Set up the "trip wires" using empty tennis ball cans as supports and a section of bamboo as the top cross piece. Fill the #10 "nitro" can with finely cut confetti to avoid a wet gym floor.

Refer to *Prouty's Landing* (next page) for an alternate use of this set-up.

139

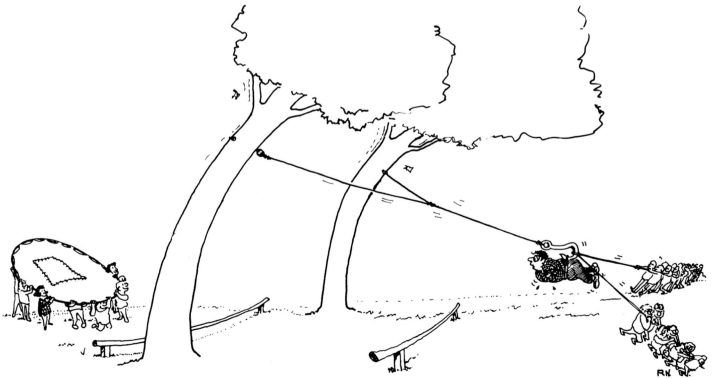

Soft Walk *

Object:

To move a group (15 folks) from a safe area, over a series of tautly strung rope sections (that traverse a putrid mass of amputated asparagus tips and artichoke hearts) to another safe area.

Tie (bowline) one end of a 100' rope (manila polypropalene, or polyester rope are best because of their minimum stretch) to a tree about three feet off the ground. Choose trees of a sturdy appearance and workable diameter. Run the rope to another tree about 8-10' away, pull the rope to make it taut, and take two round turns around the trunk at about the same height as above. Continue this routine until you run out of rope and finish off with a round turn and a couple of half hitches at the final tree.

With the natural give of the rope and the resultant slack under weight, passage on the rope by a single person is very difficult. Let a few try, to underline the difficulty.

But, if two or three persons, holding hands, make their way out on the rope, the passage becomes considerably easier, although still a challenge. This cooperative move resembles a human tension traverse.

The group moves in sections of 2-4 until the rotted delicacies are overcome. The ropes will need retightening from time to time.

To add some variation, make the last section longer (15') than the others, but offer a tension traverse rope attachment to aid balance.

Mohawk Walk ***

The Soft Walk is a good portable initiative problem, but it requires proper set-up and constant retightening of the ropes to make the problem functional. A more permanent set-up using cables can be accomplished resulting in what is now called the *Mohawk Walk*. More people can be involved at the same time and the success rate is considerably higher. The set-up is similar to the *Soft Walk* with some distance and construction variations.

Drill the support trees you have chosen for the zig-zag pattern of cables with a 5/8" drill bit about two feet off the ground. These holes are drilled all the way through the tree for insertion of the proper length bolts; as per the diameter of the tree. Sections of cable are then tightly strung between the eye bolts, using a come-along arrangement (mechanical tightening mechanism). Short swings, double cables and stumps can be used to provide variety during the various crossings.

The rules are essentially the same as in the *Soft Walk* with the following variations. Falls from the low cables are to be expected. Rather than having that person(s) return to the start, announce that each fall (touching the ground) will result in a 15 second penalty, (if the event is being timed). Another approach is to tell the group that such-and-such a number of falls will be allowed during the entire passage, and that they should try to complete the trip in the least number of falls possible. There should be some criteria of performance in order to make the participants try their best.

If I could give 4 stars, this initiative problem would be a worthy candidate; it involves everyone, concentration is intense, and laughter is abundant.

The object of this very popular initiative problem is to see how many people you can swing onto a 3'x3' platform from a starting point approx. 20' away from the platform. To determine where to place the platform, position it about 10' away from the plumb line of your swing rope (the rope can be part of a nitro crossing set up or a gymnasium climbing rope), and try a few swings to see where the starting line realistically should be located. A few trial and error swings (before the participants arrive) will give you a workable and challenging problem. To add to the challenge, put a stick (ideally, a length of bamboo) on top of two used tennis ball cans directly in front of the take-off spot. If someone inadvertently knocks the stick (tripwire) over, the entire group must begin again. Basically, follow the rules for the Nitro Crossing initiative problem.

142

If you have ever played or watched the game Skittleball, you can appreciate what happens after a number of people are perched precariously on the platform and a substantial swinger comes zinging into the group.

I Can Row a Boat, Canoe? *

Object:

To get 11 or maybe 12 adults (14 adolescents) out on a plank and into a 17' canoe that is tethered about 6' from a dock, shore, etc. without swamping—and paddle the canoe a distance of about 50' to a destination in shallow water.

Rules and Procedures:

The canoe is at first held in place by an instructor using either a boat hook (if the water is deep) or simply standing next to the canoe, until the plank is placed.

The plank (2"x8"x12') is placed from shore to the canoe by the students. The canoe should be placed so that it is possible to extend the plank slightly beyond the far gunwale.

Allow only one paddle. The paddle can be used to steady the canoe when loading but cannot touch the bottom of the pond, lake, etc.

Considerations:

If this initiative problem is attempted in water over 4' deep, do not allow anyone to put his/her legs under the seats or thwarts. This activity does not lend itself to cold weather attempts unless you are trying for an inordinate amount of stress or are developing a practical hypothermic first aid situation.

Introduction to STUNTS

Nicki Hall

This chapter represents a grab bag of useable activities that don't fit into the other 3 categories: STUNTS reads better than MISCELLANEOUS. But don't dismiss the contents of this section as an amended appendage included to fill white space—some of these "quickies" are 3 star gems.

Snowflake ***

"The simplest are the funnest."

Get hold of some loose styrofoam packing material; say a small box full. These ultra lightweight objects are your "snowflakes." Did you know that no two pieces of styrofoam are ever exactly alike? No, really ... that's true; I read it somewhere.

Climb to the top of something (staging, tree, ladder, astrodome) and launch a snowflake or two. Watch their slow and erratic descent. I'll bet it would be tough for a person down below to catch one on his/her tongue. Oral adventure at its best. Be careful not to inhale/choke on a snowflake.

This activity is not recommended for younger students, particularly pre-school, who might attempt to ingest a temptingly chewable piece of foam.

Note from the U.S.D.A.—Dispose of all tongued styrofoam pieces because of inevitable hygienic concerns. If your floor area is "clean enough to eat off," recycle the missed "snowflakes." If the floor's cleanliness is suspect, you can play "Squash the Grub," a quaint foot-stomping survival activity indigenous to the African pygmy.

145

People - to - People Surfing *

Situate the group (as many as possible) lying face down on a grassy area so that bodies are parallel to one another and about two feet apart. If you have a grassy area available on a slightly downward incline, use it; the surfer travels faster and usually farther.

Ask a volunteer surfer to lie face down, at right angles and on top of the first two or three bodies on the surf. As the entertainment director shouts "Surf's up," the people under the surfer roll over in a direction that everyone has agreed upon—downhill is certainly easier. If the surf machine is well-controlled, the surfer will travel swiftly (albeit somewhat lumpily) toward the "beach." Each member of the "surf" performs one roll as soon as the surfer reaches him/her. Resituate the surf mechanism and repeat with another "Hot Curl" sequence for the next malahini.

Paper Core Surfing *

This event is more in line with a pure stand-up-hang-ten surfing technique. It's as close to real surfing as can be accomplished on a gym floor; which isn't saying much, but...

To achieve Hodad Surf status, you must acquire a number (say 15) of paper cores. Paper cores are the inner cores of large paper rolls. Our local source of these cores is the International Paper Company in Framingham, MA. They are apparently throw-away items, so check your local paper manufacturing companies for these essential playthings. The ones we use measure 24" long by 12" in diameter, and can easily support the weight of a person.

Arrange 10-15 of these cores on the gym floor so that they are about 18" apart (roller-to-roller, not end-to-end). Then place a 2'x4' section of ½" plywood lengthwise on top of the first two rollers. This piece of plywood should have the corners and edges beveled and be well sanded to remove splinters.

The group lines up on both sides of the situated rollers to prevent wipeouts (basic spotting). The surfer jogs a few strides to gain momentum and jumps on the "surfboard" with a practiced double-footed leap, and rides the rollers—to the end if possible. There is obviously some risk associated with this activity, so spot carefully and prevent wild, uncontrolled leaps onto the board.

Core Surfing on Foam *

In order to set up a safer, though somewhat slower surf sequence, replace the plywood board, as above, with an identically-sized piece of foam padding: the kind most gyms have around to prevent bumps and bruises.

Instead of leaping onto this pad, step gingerly aboard and grasp the offered rope. The other end of the rope is held down-gym by a group of eager pullers who provide the impetus for your ride. The cores in this case, are set closer together (4"-6" apart); and spotting is still necessary.

Experiment a bit with speed and distance and I think you will be pleased with the it's-my-turn results.

Surf Massage *

If you're not into breakneck surfing, how about a surf massage? Place the rollers about 12" apart and ask someone to lie on his/her back so that the head is directed toward the destination. Remaining rigidly prone, the massagee is propelled forward by two pushers, each pushing on a foot. There is a unique bumpity-bump-bump sensation resulting from this propulsion that is quite unlike anything on the market.

If you want to make this a group initiative problem, try moving a participant on top of the rollers (as above) the full length of a gym using only 15 rollers. An assembly line (bucket brigade) must be quickly and efficiently established so that as soon as a core is used up, it must be brought to the front, set down, and aligned, before the rider's head reaches that point. Be sure to have two spotters watching the rider's head and torso in case the group pushes faster than they are able to "lay track."

Balance Practice **

Remember how, at a circus, the clown would balance plates or a chair at the end of a long pole that was planted on the chin or forehead of the performer? That type of balance skill takes a lot of practice, and more time (or patience) than you have available with a group. But, try some small-scale balancing "tricks" using a 1" x 3" wooden dowel. (Use an old broom or mop handle.) Almost everyone can gain some immediate success and satisfaction from balancing such a rod in a vertical position on the palm of his/her hand. These balance attempts require some hand, arm and body movement and, in some cases, jogging this way and that to keep the rod from falling, but that's fun and given to repetition.

As skill or luck increases, try balancing the rod on your chin, forehead or even your nose. Have different lengths of dowel material available and increase the length of the balance rod (broom handle) for a greater challenge. Contests for maximum vertical time aloft or distance covered while balancing are natural incentives for continued practice.

Orange Teeth **

Try this simple stunt and listen to the "how-do-you-do-that?" comments. It's a good lunch-time diversion.

Cut an orange (the tough, thin-skinned oranges work best) into quarters and eat the edible part down to the whitish rind. Take a knife and cut the peel as indicated in the photo below, to form "teeth."

Position the rind in your mouth so that the exterior (orange color) of the peel faces in, and fit the edges of the rind between your lips and gums.

Your noticeably ascorbic false teeth are then in place. Stick your tongue through the "teeth" for a touch of bizzare realism.

This idea is straight from the 4th grade via my son, Matthew. From the mouths of babes...

Flubber Ball *

Seat Spin *

Take the ball and run with it—if you can catch it. Inject your favorite inflatable sport ball with a heady dose of helium. Your ball won't float away, but the results are noticeable.

If the ball is made of lightweight material or is thin-walled, the ball will react more dramatically to the helium—the ultimate thin-walled/lightweight ball being, of course, a balloon.

I suspect helium help is against somebody's formal rules, so beware of using your flubber ball in sanctioned win/lose games.

I wonder how a cage ball would handle if filled with helium?

If your group is into spinning, ask each person to try this simple maneuver. Sit on the gym floor (the slipperier, the better), and throw or thrust your extended legs to the right or left in order to initiate a spin on your buttocks. As soon as the spin has started, tuck your knees and arms up to your chest to feel the immediate acceleration and rapid spin rate; a la figure skaters. If you can hold two revolutions before tipping over, you are doing well.

This simplistic spin-a-roo stunt does not work well on asphalt (hot top).

The world's record for gluteal spinning is held by Tillie Haversac, who in 1957 spun around 13 times before losing her All-American lunch (hot dog, large coke, and a Twinkie). Awesome!

148

The Ten Member Pyramid **

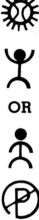

Object:

To build a symmetrical pyramid with a group of ten people as quickly and efficiently as possible.

Consideration:

In your presentation, make no mention of having to form the pyramid with all participants on their hands and knees. The problem can be solved and performed in less than 5 seconds by a group that simply lies down or lines up in the assigned 4-3-2-1 sequence—that's initiative—that's thinking! Basically sneaky, but acceptable.

Rules:

1. If possible the group should be co-ed.
2. Timing begins when the problem has been given and ends when the final person tops off the horizontal or vertical apex.
3. The exercise should be done either on mats in the gym or outside on soft ground.
4. Only a 4-3-2-1 person pyramid is considered symmetrical.

Note: This problem lends itself to a discussion about decision-making, leadership, and cooperative effort.

The problem of physically stacking 10 people points out that an initial, often frenetic, burst of activity often is not the best approach. As a group attempts to solve an initiative problem, the first suggestion is often accepted as the only solution. The team "puts on the blinders" and, in a flurry of physical maneuvers, forgets to think. Some level of thoughtful planning should be necessary to achieve an efficient solution.

149

The Mobile Ten Person Pyramid *

15 Person Pyramid *

While watching the *Guiness Book of World Records* TV show some time ago, I saw a group of talented young girls (and one boy) build a ten person pyramid and travel (crawl) 25′ in 32.8 seconds: a new world's record (the old record was 35+ seconds).

The 10 person pyramid is a great way to show a group that there is "more than one way to skin a cat." To further the fun, use the record established above as a functional touchstone for your group's attempt. As a concession to knees and noses, use a wrestling mat for your record attempt.

People love to break (or attempt to break) records. An unknown group from western wherever is the best team to topple. Pitting yourself against a distant and unknown opponent precludes the negative head-to-head consequences of you-win, I-lose contests. When it's all over, not many really care (beyond 5 minutes) if a record is set, becoming involved much more with the enjoyment of the attempt(s).

After a group has tried the 10 person pyramid and whatever discussion that results has been concluded, ask 15 volunteers to try and construct a people pyramid (an actual, on-your-hands-and-knees pyramid): 5-4-3-2-1.

Being five kneelers high, the participants will have to organize themselves by size and commitment potential, since the top person could be over 10 ft. off the ground. Use observers as spotters.

Considering the elevation of this potential pyramid and the number of bodies involved, the construction problem itself seems enough of a challenge without adding time expectations. Use a wrestling mat.

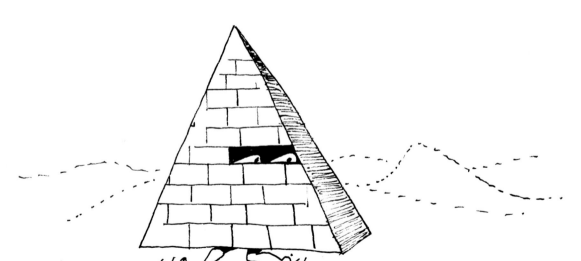

The Rope Push *

Halve your group and ask each half to stand on either side of a marker line (chalk line or rope). Hand them a 60-80 ft. length of rope (any diameter or material) so that each team has an equal amount of rope on their side of the marker line. Mark the center of the rope with a piece of tape. At this juncture, your listeners are probably anticipating a Tug-of-War, but the object this time is, at the end of a one minute time limit, to have more of your rope on the opposite side than they have of their rope on your side! WHAT? Right, this is a rope push, not pull. Here are a couple of rules to ease the transition from tradition to chaos.

No one on either team is allowed to cross over and touch the other team's turf or person (no purposeful contact). Tugging on the rope is tabu—only push. Throwing the rope is allowed.

Judging this event is well nigh impossible, but who cares? A tie is usually well received by everyone except the most diehard competitors. This confused melee of people and rope is sometimes worth trying again, so suggest taking a minute or two to develop team strategies, subterfuges, and sneaky initiative ideas.

151

Bob Nilson

Warm-Ups

Getting a participant warmed up at the beginning of an activity session seems necessary (hours of academia on your backside is enough to make anyone's circulatory system sluggish) and generally proves troublesome—not many people want to be warmed up. So, your initial cardio-vascular sequence should be active and unique. Being active is no problem. The take-a-lap-and-come-back-here-for-instructions approach has been used and abused for years. But, providing initial and satisfying variety of movement requires thought, inventiveness, daily commitment, and compassion.

Here are a few warm-up ideas that have been used randomly (not repetitively) and which have been well received by most people.

Tag Games

You played some kind of tag games when you were a kid, right? You had to! It's a prerequisite of growing up: a physical and social obligation. Take those "ancient" good games, change the rules and lingo a bit to fit the group and occasion, and see how usable they become as unique warm-ups.

Tag is an ideal warmer-upper because the games are very active, the rules are few, and play doesn't have to last a predictable length of time. Play until enthusiasm wanes and then either change games or move on to another activity. If an individual doesn't want to be *too* active, most tag games allow self-elimination.

Everybody's It ***

Often called, "The World's Fastest Tag Game" and rightly so, because everyone is literally IT. As in any tag game, if someone is IT, they chase someone else; so in this case, everyone's chasing someone else. Here's a couple of rules to put this confusion in context.

The group spreads out within a bounded area (the boundaries have been previously set) and at the GO signal, each person attempts to tag someone else. If a tag is received (before you tag the tagger), you are eliminated. Sit down or put your hands on your head to indicate your "tagged" status. If you were lucky or skillful enough to be the tagger, continue trying to eliminate other players. This fast action continues until only one player remains. Then just as he/she begins to congratulate him/herself on being champion, shout GO again, and the action begins afresh.

If the last few players are more cautious than confident, the game may drag as they try to avoid one another. To initiate action, announce that anyone who takes a backward step is eliminated: aggression is immediate.

153

Sore Spot Tag/ Hospital Tag **

Same rules as above except the tapped person must hold the spot where he/she was tagged (with one hand) until he/she tags someone else. The game is made considerably more difficult by requiring the tagged person to hold the spot with both hands, leaving only the head to tag with. If you took that last rule seriously you're being too serious. The handicap and good humored embarassment of a tag varies considerably as to where the tag is affixed. It's hard to keep from laughing if the tag was on your posterior, and trying to run with a tag on your foot is a frustrating task.

A variation of this tag game that resembles *Everybody's It* involves continuing, after having been tagged, by holding the tagged spot with one hand. Since everyone is IT, there is a good chance that you will soon be tagged again and, of course, have to hold that spot with your free hand. As in the Monty Python comedy sequence involving the truculent, truncated knight, you may continue until your multi-tagged carcass is a quivering mass of touched spots. How far to go with this variation is up to your sense of humor and the group's ability to handle "Holy Grail" humor.

Foetal Tag *

This tag game allows some practice with the moving front shoulder roll and thus should be played only after a learning-how-to-fall session (refer to TRUST chapter) has been presented and practiced.

The same rules as in other tag games are used except the tag must be above the waist. It's too easy to grab a foot while a shoulder roll is being done, possibly causing an injury. The immune position (5 seconds) is the foetal position, which must be' preceded by a shoulder roll. Because of the frequent self-initiated falls, this game should be played on grass, not a hard gym floor.

This tag game is best presented during the fall and roll instruction sequence because of the expertise needed to safely perform a shoulder roll from a run.

Hop On Tag *

The IT person must attempt to tag another player (one hand below the waist, two hands below the neck, three hands below the ears, whatever) at which juncture that tagged person becomes IT, the fun, as in any tag game, results from trying not to be caught, coupled with the titillating fear of the chase, or the more socially devastating situation of not being chased. The only safe area inside the boundaries (you have to have boundaries or the game quickly dissolves into a one-on-one cross-country jaunt) is on someone's back or body (dorsal or ventral). This piggyback or front position grants a five second immunity to the pair, at the end of which time they must separate and run to find another partner to hop on or be hopped on. A player may not hop on the same individual twice in succession. If the group is larger than fifteen individuals or so, designate two people as being IT to speed things up. With two people simultaneously being IT, they must do something to identify themselves, such as making a continuous sound or running about holding one hand over their head, etc.

Triangle Tag **

A hand-held triangular game for four people. Use this as a quickie warm-up activity.

Ask your group to quad-up in groups of four (I know that's superfluous, but....) and ask three of the participants to hold hands forming a triangle. One member of the triangle is the person designated to be caught, and the other two are blockers or protectors. The fourth person is IT and must try to tag the designated odd person in the triangle. The IT can run around the triangle and try to jump across the triangle, but cannot purposefully try to break a grip. The triangle personnel dance and jump about in semi-coordinated moves to keep the IT at bay. Change roles in a clockwise direction every 60 seconds or when a catch is made. (Or, never change positions and play the same rules every day for two weeks to measure your classes' potential for civil disobedience.)

Flip-Me-the-Bird Tag* Ⓟ

Tie knots in old towels to equal half the number of people in the group. These knotted towels are called *birds*. If your budget and sense of humor allows, buy rubber chickens (about $6.00 each) to equal half the number of people...etc.

Assign 2-3 people to be IT. To be immune from a tag, a player must be grasping a bird. Since there are only 8 birds to 16 pursuees, there is much throwing of the bird. There can only be one bird in the hand. In keeping with the name of the game, the bird cannot be thrown to the same person twice in succession. Use restricted boundaries as mentioned previously in other tag game instructions.

Dizzy Izzy Tag *

Same basic tag rules as above (without the hopping ingredient), but after being tagged, a new IT must spin around three times before chasing another person. This vertigo pause prevents "tag backs," a heavy rule refinement in serious tag games.

Two in a Row **

Using a piece of retired climbing rope (a 75' section will do nicely) as a jump rope, ask a group to see how many people can make two consecutive jumps together without anyone missing. Starting position—rope on the floor or ground and everyone standing on one side of the rope. Turning direction and standing position is up to the group. Twenty people is challenging, but certainly not impossible. Considering that on a missed jump the rope ends up tangled around someone's ankle, knee or worse, it's humorously obvious who missed.

Change "turners" occasionally to combat arm fatigue and to keep a consistent turn and arc. To be an effective and constant turner is a valued street skill. To alert the jumping group of an imminent turn, one of the rope turners loudly announces, "READY—TURN," followed immediately by an attempt.

156

Peter Steele

The Turnstile ***

Using the same section of rope as above, begin turning at a slow rate and ask the group to see if they can *all* get through the spinning rope from one side to another by (1) going through one at a time; (2) making one jump while in the arc; (3) not missing a beat of the rope between people. Not a hard assignment for one person or two or three, but it can prove to be a frustrating challenge for 20 or 30 people. Don't let frustration stop the attempt; I've yet to see a group not succeed eventually in getting everyone through. Provide the necessary time to allow many attempts.

Double Dutch *

Using the same section of rope as above, double it and subtract some rope so that each section is about 20' long. With one section in each turner's hand, have them spin a "Double Dutch" tattoo on the floor or street. If you don't know what Double Dutch is, ask any streetwise student for a demonstration, because verbalizing the sequence is harder than trying it. This is the stuff of pure nostalgia for some, an aesthetic and physical awakening to others, and flagellating frustration for most. I have seen young women perform feats of endurance and skill among, on top of, and underneath those spinning double ropes that would make a *Sports Illustrated* photographer's index finger itch. Try stepping into those whirling ropes for a little "hot pepper"; it's a humbler!

Using this difficult jump rope sequence often allows some students to display an impressive level of individual performance that they are not capable of in more traditional sports and games. Strokes and ego burnishing—we all need it.

Invisible Jump Rope ***

There *is* a reason why boxers jump rope: it is an effective (and somewhat boring) cardio-vascular exercise. Jumping rope is not, as I was lead to believe as an adolescent, just an innocuous pastime for sweet-young-things. If you continue to think that a twirling rope is a bit on the tweeky side, try hopping into a staccato-like hot pepper, double dutch set-up for a bit of humble pie. Most students (male and female) respond well to jumping rope in its many forms, if presented as a means of achieving fitness coordination and having fun.

As you watch an adept jumper windmill his/her way through a complex routine of cross-overs, jig-like steps and double jumps, the uncomfortable knowledge that tripping over your own feet is easy enough suggests that you don't need a rope to complicate things. In other words, you need a warm-up routine that will allow you to emulate the good guys without having to look bad. (The only time that it's OK to look bad is when everyone is looking bad, and even then it's a strain on chronically pumped-up egos.)

So, just pretend. Measure the length of your pretend rope by standing on the rope and bringing the ends up under your armpits. You can't expect to do all the following tricks if your pretend rope is too short! Step off the rope (the one you were just measuring) and, holding the ends, flip the bight over your head. *Nobody* begins jumping with the rope in front.

Begin slowly, jumping and casually turning the rope in sequence with your hops. See how easy it is to coordinate the hand and foot movements.

Try a trick! Cross your hands (and your arms up to your elbows) vigorously in front of you each time you jump. This crossover move isn't that difficult and will definitely impress your friends. Try a double crossover. Nicely done, and not a miss yet.

You of course, recognize by now that almost anything is possible within this existential format, so use your imagination—here are a few starters for this anything-goes workout.

1. Try a double jump, a triple...then six turns with one jump. If you make it, you have just broken the world's record. (Five turns in one jump is the record—no kidding.)

2. Try some fancy footwork, any old dance step that you can think of will do; a jig, a fling, an entrechat, etc.

3. Entice someone near you to jump at your pace and initiate "follow the leader." At the end of a few wildly impossible moves, hop away from one another and at a wink, both throw the ropes high in the air toward your distant partner. Grasp the falling, flailing rope and continue jumping without missing a beat. Fantastic!

4. Hop toward someone and jump as a pair, entertwining each other's rope so that your feat is as impossible as it is delightful.

5. End with some kind of Brogdingagian group jump—and not one person has missed a beat. Hot pepper!

Inch Worm **

Sit on the turf facing your partner. Inch toward one another until you and he or she are close enough to sit on each other's feet. Big feet offer an advantage or at least a certain comfort factor. Grasp your partner's elbows or upper arms with each hand.

Now decide which direction you two would like to travel. Lateral movement is out, so it's either north or south, east or west or...you know what I mean. After deciding, the partner (in whose direction you're headed) lifts her/his derriere off the ground and moves 12 inches or so toward whatever goal you have in mind: be reasonable. The second partner now lifts off the ground and in a cooperative, bug-like movement duplicates the step above and moves toward his/her partner.

A natural exercise for impromptu, disjointed competition.

158

Bottoms Up **

A one-on-one warm-up exercise that combines strength, balance and a very odd position.

Sit on the turf facing one another and place the bottom of your feet against the bottom of your partner's feet. Legs should be bent, feet held high, and posteriors skootched fairly close to one another. Then attempt to push against your partner's feet (while putting all your weight on your arms), until both of your derrieres come off the ground. You will notice (poignantly) a tightening of the tricep muscles in your arms, considerable laughter, and not much movement on the first couple of tries.

If your bottom remains permanently welded to the ground, blame it on your partner and find someone more your size to blame the next time.

Candle *

A somewhat stylized exercise that promotes concentration and balance awareness. With one foot on the ground, tuck the other foot as far on the inside of the opposite thigh as possible; sole of foot on thigh. Balance here momentarily (like a Masi warrior) to get the feel of this precarious stance and then, with palms opposed in a praying position, raise the hands slowly and vertically to an overhead position. Think of the hands, passing eye level, as a light being flicked to the OFF position. Ask the delicately-postured students to maintain this eye-closed position for 15 seconds. Try the other foot now placed on the opposite thigh and remember, Masi warriors had a spear to lean on.

Mini Balance Test *

After performing the Candle concentration/balance exercise, participants might be interested in a quick, self-graded balance test.

Have all the students stand separately, a few feet apart, and raise up on their tip-toes (way up). The arms are then extended together to the front, so that the student looks ready to begin a dive. The feet should be placed close together. Try to hold this tippy position for 30 seconds with eyes closed, without falling from the on-toes, feet-together stance. If someone topples, indicate that he/she should return immediately to the previous balanced posture. If each participant counts the number of times a balance lapse occurs, a means for future comparison is recorded. If some students want to cheat a little in order to make themselves feel better or build their status amongst their peers (or impress you)—why not? The result of this test is not research data material.

5-5-5 Duo Isometrics **

1. Facing one another and with arms extended, ask students to put both hands on each other's shoulders. (Try this exercise with a partner of near equal height.) Partners gradually begin trying to push each other into the ground. Increase pressure over a 5-second time span, maintain full pressure for about 5 seconds and then gradually decrease pressure for about 5 seconds until back to normal. Ask one of the partners to count aloud in order to regulate and coordinate pressure applied.

To increase the commitment and enjoyment, ask the two participants to maintain eye contact throughout the exercise.

2. Facing one another, have students extend one hand forward as if they were going to shake their partner's hand. Keeping hands open and flat (not clasped) and with arms extended, begin to exert lateral pressure on a partner's arm using the 5-5-5 second counting pattern as in (1). This is not as a contest; so don't allow students to twist their bodies to gain a leverage advantage. Partners should remain laterally parallel to each other at all times. If done well, both students' hands should not move side-to-side more than an inch. The increased, maintained and decreasing pressure is a satisfying feeling.

There are numerous spatial variations to this cooperative-exercise sequence. Ask the students to use their imaginations to come up with other 5-5-5 isometric exercise postions. Don't forget the use of legs.

161

** Red Baron Stretch

Pretend that each of your hands (salute position) is an airplane engaging in an aerial dogfight. Right hand—Red Baron; Left-hand—Snoopy. The "planes" can chase each other anywhere that your body and arm movements allow. Keep your feet comfortably separated and stationary.

Don't forget to add the oral gunfire sounds so natural to this exercise. To add a bit of cooperation to the "dogfight," ask one person to be the "Red Baron" and the other to be "Snoopy." Right hand to left hand, for example. All movements must be in slow motion so that the participants can stay in sync with one another. This is a zany, come-join-me-in-play stretching exercise and not meant to be competitive.

Stork Stretch *

Do a few back-of-the-leg warm-up activities and individual limberness exercises before trying this triad stretch.

Split into groups of three. Stand facing each other in a triangular configuration. One person raises his/her right leg and places the right foot on the right thigh of the person to their right, as that person continues the identical action to their right. Right! So, it's everyone's right leg as parallel to the ground as possible, as the right leg is supported on the righthand partner's thigh.

The left legs (3 of them in most groups) support the trio. After achieving this unique balanced position, all try to lean over and place their head on their right knee, (or depending upon the triangular rapport, on their partner's knee). As you attempt this movement, a certain tightening of the hamstrings will occur, accompanied by various deep-throated gutteral sounds.

This "stretcher" is not designed for everyone's body, but the cooperative results are worth an attempt.

Chronological Line- Up

Line up by age to the nearest year, month, day. The advantage of using this method is that it allows the participants to say something about themselves that is normally a withheld fact and spoken of only jokingly. This rookie-to-venerable line works particularly well with an adult group exhibiting a wide age span.

Alternate #1: Ask the group to perform the above task non-verbally.

Alternate #2: Ask the group to line up as above, non-verbally and blindfolded. Start as a blindfolded cluster. This seemingly improbable task can be accomplished rather quickly by some groups—other groups have been known to miss dinner.

Briefly: Line up or assemble groups by: Your sign (horoscope); the number of teeth you have missing (or left); hair shades (real or fabricated); shoe sizes; belt size; last number of your phone number; make of your car; your wife or girl friend's middle initial, etc.

Looking for two approximately equal numbered groups? Or some controversy? Separate the group into two parts by:

1. Last name starts with A-M or N-Z.
2. Pants or jacket color.
3. Coffee drinker or not?
4. Cigarette smoker?
5. Do you put left or right foot in your pants first?
6. Hands folded—is the right or left thumb on top?
7. Like or dislike—Howard Cosell (or any other controversial, well-known personality)? Be prepared for some good-natured comments during this pairing up.
8. Rather take a shower or bath (strong male/female separation).
9. Birthday in Dec.-May or June-November.
10. Coffee or tea with or without sugar—non-coffee drinkers even out the groups.

The Balance Broom **

The Balance Broom is an activity that is fun but also results in subtle improvements in commitment and a willingness to appear "uncool" in front of others. How many young and older people miss out on available learning situations because they don't want to appear foolish or inept before their peers?

Procedure:

Ask a participant to hold a broom vertically (a stick or foam sword serves as well) with the handle directly over his/her head and look up at the very top of the broom. Ask the participant to perform fifteen 360° turns with his/her arm vertically extended, and then attempt to put the broom down on the ground and step over its length. While turning, the participant should keep his/her eyes open and fixed at the top of the broom.

Most spinners will fall before reaching fifteen turns, and the remainder will experience difficulty stepping over the broom handle. The value of the exercise lies mainly in two areas: (1) It is a stunt that most people will have trouble completing thus exposing themselves to failure. This potentially negative experience lessens normal sensitivity to failure because the activity is fun and the group, engrossed in the enjoyment of the moment, is laughingly supportive of any effort, no matter how inept. The exercise can be kept from degenerating into a negative experience by the control that the instructor maintains on the event and the people involved. (2) Successful completion does require concentration and concerted effort. Dizziness can be controlled by most people.

There is potential for injury if this event is not spotted well by 3-4 people. Some "spinners" become so disoriented that when they fall to the ground, their bodies are not prepared (spatially oriented) for the jolt and injuries have resulted.

As a spotter, do not attempt to keep a person upright, but cushion a fall when it occurs. Also, do not immediately let go of a disoriented person. Although his/her body has stopped turning, the inner ear fluid is still rotating.

Contraindications:

Announce what this activity involves and the physical disorientation (dizziness) that results. Some people are prone to nausea (motion sickness) if they become dizzy and this unsettled condition may last for hours.

Dizziness has been reported to trigger epileptic attacks.

Hang Ten Climbing Posts ** ☼

These buried-in-the-ground tree limbs and trunks provide a series of physical tasks that appeal to the more adventurous participant or someone who appreciates a demanding personal challenge.

The challenge provided by these vertically placed posts is twofold: (1) See if you can get to the top of a post by yourself and stand unaided (balanced) for five seconds. During this attempt, anything goes, as long as it's just you against gravity; i.e., no props allowed.

(2) A more finely tuned and classic challenge is available by assigning 10 quality points to the climber before an attempt is made, and then asking the climber to maintain those points during the climb as a "master climber" observes and subtracts points for miscalculations, slips and poor moves.

For the aspiring rock climber, gymnast, or agile student, such graded attempts can become addictive. The posts also provide a fine workout for anyone with the gumption to try. Since you (imbued with pedagogic largesse) are grading the climbs, there should be satisfaction aplenty for those who need it.

Scoring details—Subtract a point (or ½ point) each time someone: (a) puts his/her hand on the climbing post above eye level, (b) touches the post with feet or hands and subsequently slips or makes a scrambling movement.

Add a point for any spectacular move or for noteworthy endurance. Be sparing with added points, however, and keep the 10 points maximum as a rarely achieved pinnacle. People like an unattainable goal occasionally.

Placing the half-dozen or so "posts" that make up this event is usually easier than procuring the cut sections. You will need:

1. 3-6' and 10-12' sections of 5" to 10" diameter cut tree limbs or trunks. Try to include a bifurcated Y section at the top of one post for variety.
2. Your trusty PHD (post hole digger) and shovel.
3. 2-3 gals. creosote.
4. A chain saw or large bow saw.
5. A 6' cut limb of 2" diameter to act as a tamper.

Pick a flat, grassy area for this event. Do not choose a landfill site, because digging is predictably difficult.

Strip off all bark with a draw knife from the cut posts to accelerate drying and retard insect damage. Posts may be painted with Penta (wood preservative) after drying in situ for a couple of months.

Begin digging your holes so that the posts will be far enough apart to allow efficient spotting. Holes should be 3-3½' deep. Pour some creosote in the bottom of the hole before placing the stump. Also, pour some creosote at the dirt/stump interface after the pole hole has been filled in and tamped. The creosote significantly reduces the rate of decay in the wood.

Do not paint creosote on that part of the pole to be climbed. Creosote and skin do not get along well.

Tamp the dirt in firmly around the pole to prevent the wobblies.

Using a chain saw, cut small notches in the poles to act as climbing holds. Make them large (2") or small (½"), depending upon the desired degree of difficulty. Take advantage of limb stumps to act as foot and hand holds—trim to size.

165

Popsicle Push-Up ***

This cooperative activity can be used as a simple four-person stunt, or you can continue to add people ending up with a useful large group initiative problem.

To set up the initial four-person attempt, ask for four volunteers, who can do at least one push-up. Ask one person to lie face down on the ground, as if preparing to do a push-up. The second person lies face down, at right angles to the first person so that the tops of his/her feet are on top of the first person's lower back. The third person repeats the procedure, using the second person as their foot rest. The fourth person fits in this weave so as to connect everyone in a square configuration. All four should be face down with their instep on someone's back.

On a signal, everyone does a push-up. If done together, there will be four raised bodies, with only eight hands touching the ground: simple but impressive.

If one of the participants has trouble getting up (foot pressure on their back might cause a problem), tell him/her that you will give a 1-2-GO COUNT, and that the "permanently prone" individual should attempt a push-up on the count of two, offering the advantage of a head start.

After your groups of four have had some fun with this quartet push-up (including a 360° rotation attempt while in the up position—doomed for failure, but worth a laugh or two), ask the group to continue to add people to one of the quad arrangements in an attempt to include the whole group (4 to infinity) in a mass popsicle push-up. There is more than one solution.

This problem is time-consuming—not from the standpoint of discovering a workable solution, but because it takes a long time for a group to decide on a technique and implement it. This group attempt needs a leader.

People who cannot do a push-up or have back problems can be official photographers or prejudiced referees for this WORLD'S RECORD attempt.

Pole (Sapling) Vaulting **

Simple field vaulting is a spontaneous, just-fooling-around activity that generates a good upper body workout and a sense of risk-taking that encourages continued efforts. In addition, vaulting is physically satisfying and doing it is much more exciting than watching. There really is a sense of weightlessness and swift movement that can be achieved with a simple vaulting pole (sturdy, please—no mop handles or skinny bamboo poles).

Provide a number of hardwood sapling sections (about 8') that will support *your* weight (i.e.; try them out), to big or little folks in a grassy area. Ask them to vault from place to place. This is done simply by jogging forward, placing the pole in the turf (a la TV's Wide World of Sports) and vaulting. I'm not going to burden you with a detailed or anytailed explanation of the kinesiology of vaulting, and you shouldn't have to explain, either. If the pole is planted solidly and a person thrusts forward from that juncture, forward progress, free of the ground, will occur. If not, there's plenty of time, grass, iced tea, and tries left.

If the vaulting pole continues to end up between a person's legs, you might want to assist with some basic technique suggestions like: "Don't let the pole go between your legs."

If rapidly gained expertise indicates a desire for self-testing, set up a vault for distance over grass, sand or even a small gully. If the situation presents itself, don't ignore a wet or muddy area as incentive for a grand challenge.

Dog Shake *

If the group has been working with you for a couple of weeks and they obviously need or are in the mood for a bit of shared nonsense, tell them (at the beginning of your session) that you have an exercise designed to physically loosen up a group.

Don't present this exercise until the group has had a chance to figure you out. You may want to practice the following routine a few times before demonstrating it. Pick your practice site wisely.

The Dog Shake takes its name directly from the way a dripping wet dog shakes himself (right next to you), kinetically demonstrating a biologically ideal way to initiate the drying process. You will never be able to duplicate the unhinged explosive wiggling movements that a dog achieves, but in relative slow motion, the human miming attempts are fun and uninhibiting.

To convince an understandably dubious group to join you in a Dog Shake is largely dependent upon the instructor's charisma and/or acting ability, for he/she must initially demonstrate the moves including a running and sometimes garbled commentary which goes something like this: "A dog's shake always begins at the tip of the nose." (Begin wiggling nose.) "It's hard to wiggle the nose without including the cheeks and mouth." (Exaggerate mouth and cheek movements. It's good for a laugh.) "If you are worried about what other people are thinking of you, relax, because here go the eyes." (Roll your eyes randomly in their sockets. Now, move smoothly (?) and consistently down from one body part to another.) "The whole head begins to bounce around, which starts the shoulders to moving and then the arms can't help bobbing about." "Don't forget the head and eyes." "The chest is part of the shoulder movement, which goes right on down to the waist and hips." (If you have never done the hula, here's your chance: much exaggerated hip gyrations.)

"Are you into it?" "Can you feel the water flying off your body?" "The thighs are next, which starts the knees." (Move those knees, while keeping everything else going, of course. By this time, you are nearly 100% convulsive.) "And

then finish it off to the toes." "We made it—now, don't stop." "Do it—do it—do it." Continue a complete shaking for about five seconds or so.

People are usually laughing and obviously enjoying your antics at this point. Don't give them time to lose the laughter; ask them to join you in a Dog Shake sequence and immediately begin as above. Talk them through and join them in the Shake. The whole sequence should take no more than 60 seconds.

At the finish, shakers usually applaud themselves—a nice gesture really, there should be more of it; i.e., more opportunities which allow that type of relaxed freedom and spontaneous self-approval. After this first effort, demonstrate a complete Dog Shake. Start your nose twitching and let the movement transfer immediately and directly to your hips—kind of an impulse, manifested in a torso twitch and subtle hip shake. It's hard to verbalize but try, and if the movement feels good, it's probably right.

Ask the group to do a quickie shake with you a couple of times and applaud their actions (no matter what spasmodic efforts are forthcoming). Move on to the next exercise amidst a feeling of shared spontaneity.

Funny Face *

Afer having experienced the *Mirror Image* and *Anti-Mirror* activities, *Funny Face* is a natural and often hilarious follow-up sequence that produces some of the most grotesque facial contortions experienced since the 3rd grade.

Split your large group into smaller encounter circles, say 5-7 per silly set. The rules, recently established and constantly being ammended, state that after the GO signal everyone in the circle tries to make the other members smile. If you slip and show the slightest smile you are eliminated, and can then step back and watch the experts do their thing. A participant is not allowed to touch another player, and all eyes must stay open, otherwise anything goes.

Nicki Hall

Peter Steele

169

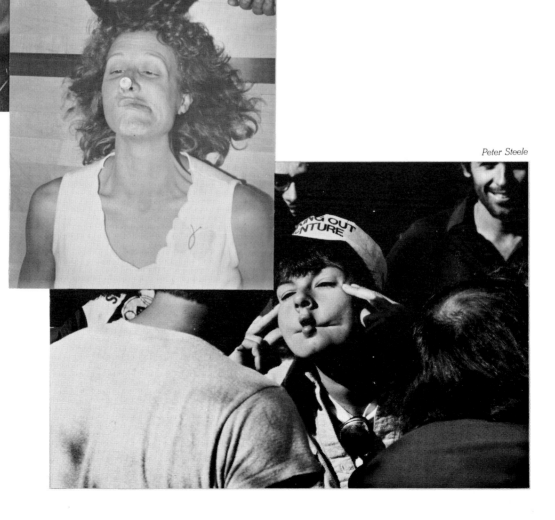

Mirror Image **

Facial and anatomical gymnastics that result are indescribable.

When the group is reduced to the last two or three, stop the action and announce that these stone-faced competitors are the regional champs and will go against the other regional champions (whoever is left from one of the other smaller encounter circles) in a faceoff. This final faceoff can result in some classic moves and reactions.

Don't approach this activity seriously. (Can it be done?) The value of funny face lies in the spontaneous reactions of the players and the unselfconscious participation that generally results. People, particularly adults, like to have an excuse to be silly occasionally.

Cooperation, unselfconscious stretching, people-to-people action: all a part of the activity *Mirror Image*.

Ask two participants to face one another, almost toe-to-toe. One person acts as the initiator and the other becomes his/her mirror image. The instructor must remember during the presentation that this activity is not competitive and that the intention is to make movements that are both interesting and slow enough to mime by the person attempting to mirror the actions. The enjoyment level of performing these cooperative actions is largely dependent on (1) the instructor's low key presentation of the activity; (2) the often zany actions that are initiated; (3) the level of cooperation between the two participants; (4) keeping the action in slow motion.

After each partner has had a chance to be initiator and follower, ask them to try the anti-mirror set up, during which sequence the follower tries to do exactly the opposite of the person starting the movements. This switch can produce some classic moves and laughable confusion. Basic rules and guidelines:

(1) Partners cannot touch one another.
(2) ALL movements must be in slow motion.
(3) One foot must remain on the ground at all times.

170

Miniature Monuments *

The object is to build the smallest possible monument. The group that accomplishes this task within a reasonable time limit gets to knock down everyone else's cairn amidst shouts of huzzah and gnashing of teeth.

Rules:

1. Each team of three is offered a pair of tweezers and a magnifying glass to help with their engineering efforts.
2. Only three chosen "stones" are allowed to be used in building the monument.
3. The monument can be built upon a piece of rock or wood only.
4. The decision of the judge(s) is final unless the other teams complain a lot, in which case victory usually goes to the loudest and most obnoxious threesome.
5. The only penalty is for inadvertent blowing over of the monuments (or parts thereof) by sniffing or sneezing. The penalty is adding one stone to the total.

Official Miniature Monument T-shirts and matching shorts are de rigueur for regional meets and are well received by knowledgeable spectators.

171

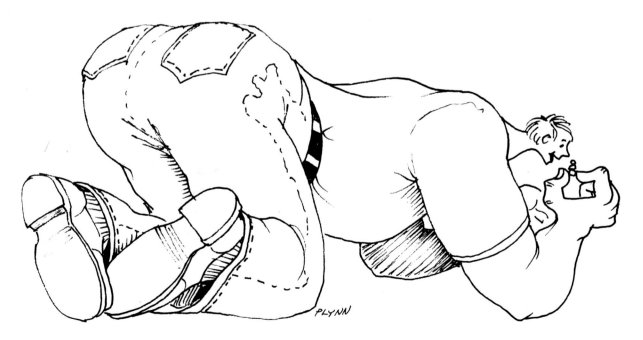

PLYNN

PDQ **

During workshops and in various educational settings, I've discovered that a sit-down session facetiously dubbed the "Play Determinant Quotient" (PDQ) Test acts as a fine deinhibitor, is good for more than a few group laughs, and clearly illustrates the instructor's role as actor and co-participant.

In your own presentation of this semi-skilled and mostly useful potpourri of shenanigans, the value extends from the participants' physical attempts to risk taking in this just-fooling-around test.

Indicate to your seated listeners that you are going to introduce, by demonstration, a progression of "things to do," and that you would like each member of the group to approximately duplicate your manipulations, sounds, movements, etc. Explain that all these nostalgic doings are self tests and are to be scored individually on a pass-fail basis. Further, indicate that the "tests" will begin easily and become progressively harder.

All of this preliminary patter is to develop interest and psych the group for trying something new, mysterious, and with a bit of pizzaz. If your earlier presentations during the workshop (class) have been effectively spontaneous, your audience (you are an impromptu actor after all) will eagerly anticipate this next bit of zaniness.

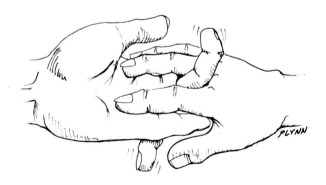

PLYNN

172

The PDQ "Test"

1. Take your right index finger and insert it into your mouth and attempt to make an oral popping sound by levering the finger of choice against the inside of your cheek and rapidly out of your mouth (keeping the lips pursed in approved manner).

Author's Note—Attempting to write about these feats of profitless dexterity is probably as tedious as reading about them. It's predictably more fun to digitally abuse your cheek than to read about it; so back to your finger and lever away. Have you ever seen someone try to "pop" their cheek and achieve only a fleshy "splooch"—it's funny and entertainingly useful in a group setting as the expert poppers attempt to aid the hapless sploochers.

1. Try the opposite finger in the other cheek; historically more difficult.

2. Snap your right finger and then the left finger, achieving a distinct snapping sound. Remember—all these performances are on a pass/fail basis. Good-naturedly emphasize the failures and jokingly remark on outstanding efforts.

3. And with the other hand and fingers, as in #2.

4. I'm not going to try to depict this next one, at least not "by the numbers." It's an age-old, two handed trick used to delight young children (and young minds) by opposing palms against one another, juxtaposing and intertwining the middle fingers, twisting the palms against one another in opposite directions (as the fingers find their way) and finally, causing the middle fingers to metronomely flip-flop in opposite directions. It is amusing to watch and fun to help someone try to accomplish this fairly intricate but well-known movement. Remember—you are to present a series of maneuvers that *will* result in occasional and obvious failure in order to share the consequences of trying something new.

5. Cup your hand and blow *across* (like across the top of a bottle or bullet shell) the small aperature formed between the second and third joint of the thumbs. This produces a hollow hooting sound that is the new-found delight of practicing youngsters and anathema to their

parents. You can extend or supplement this "test" outdoors by placing a blade of grass (wide blade for deep sounds, narrow blades for higher notes) between the thumbs (as above) and blowing directly *on* the tightly held blade. The grass acts as a reed producing a variety of animal and unearthly sounds.

6. You can finish this formal (?) part of the testing sequence by demonstrating something difficult that you can do. Try whistling loudly through your teeth. Or, touching your tongue to your nose. Or, playing a recognizable tune (I've always had good luck with "You Are My Sunshine") by cupping your hand in your arm pit under your shirt and ... you know! The folks in your group (more group than audience by this time) are usually begining to demonstrate with alacrity those ridiculous pranks that not so long ago amused their friends and aggravated their teachers and parents. A couple of tested maneuvers that have proven to be humorous and acceptably bizarre are: (a) Put your finger in either ear and seemingly extend it into your oral cavity resulting in an obvious and moveable bump in your cheek, (use your tongue please!); (b) Produce a nose-breaking sound by cupping your hands over your nose/mouth area and convincingly "pop" your nose by subtly snapping a thumbnail against your teeth.

There's no need to list more of those PDQ bizzaros because each group knows more than enough tricks to further your purposes of relaxing overly serious participants and demonstrating an engaging level of nuttiness. Even the participants who don't take part initially are drawn in by the spontaneous nature of the responses and the level of group enjoyment. This test after all is no test at all, but simply an inducement to play.

If you are looking for a no-holds-barred histrionic way to demonstrate the teacher/actor role so often used in adventure presentations, try on one of these vivid mime roles.

PLYNN

173

Balloon Blow-Up *

Lie on the floor in a fetal position with the tip of your thumb pressed against your lips. Begin blowing against your thumb, producing noticeable hissing sounds. (This is the sound of air entering the balloon—you.) Visualize your cramped body as a deflated balloon and try to think of air entering your arms and legs, and what type of movement your limbs would make as they begin to expand. Make the movements sequential and convulsively realistic. Also, be patient with the movements, remembering how long it takes to fill a large balloon.

Keep blowing and filling until your limbs begin to swell and force you into an eventual scarecrow-like standing position. Keep blowing until you are absolutely filled to your limit (cheeks puffed out, on your tip-toes, arms and legs rigid with air), and then BURST with a loud verbal POW or BANG or whatever you do best. Rapidly decrease in size, deflating toward the floor; all the while emitting loud, air-release, hissing sounds, until you end up in a heap on the floor.

A variation—Instead of bursting, simply let your air out, (a wet lip and vibrating sound) and like a balloon thus released, jet yourself willy-nilly around the room until all the propulsive air is gone.

Fried Egg Simulator *

Watch for bruises on this one; i.e., don't get carried away during the frying pan time slot.

Begin again in the fetal position, but on your knees face down toward the floor. You are, in this position, an unbroken fresh egg. To begin, ask someone to tap you (breaking your shell) and then flow onto the floor (face down, spread eagle).

Imagine an egg being broken onto a hot frying pan and try to duplicate, with body movements, the rapidly increasing formation of bubbles under the albumen; i.e., their constant formation and bursting. Can't picture it? Go fry an egg, and then be one! Use your imagination (well-honed by this time) and finish off the sequence.

To make these two mime sequences more meaningful to your audience, tell them what you are (to properly align their imaginations) but not what you are going to do—your actions should take care of that.

Dollar Jump **

Here's a stunt that almost everyone will be eager to try. If you have all your debts paid and have a spare dollar, place a dollar bill flat on the ground and tell the students that anyone who can jump over the bill lengthwise earns the dollar.

The hitch is—they must grab their toes (on both feet) by reaching over the front of their feet and not let go during the jump or landing.

Additional stipulations:

1. Players must jump forward over the length of the bill.
2. They may not fall backwards; (long jump rules are in effect).
3. Players start with their toes as close to the bill as possible. Heels must clear the vertical plane of the end of the bill after the jump, in order to be successful.

If you are strapped for funds, use a piece of paper the same size as a dollar with an IOU written on it.

Be sure to try this tricky and difficult event yourself before you start handing out cash. You may even want to put two bills end-to-end because of the shrinking dollar...

Balls Galore *

How many tennis balls can be held off the floor for five seconds by an individual standing (2 feet on the floor) after a two minute preparation time limit? Use of clothing or any other non-morphological props are not allowed for supporting the tennis balls. Also try this event with two people: one supporting the tennis balls and the other acting as a stuffer. Have at least 75 balls on hand per attempt.

Marathon Whistle *

Ask individuals in the class to see who can sustain the longest non-stop, lip-puckered whistle. Try a group whistle first to lower the commitment level and then ask for volunteers. This is obviously not a serious contest, so aim at having fun. It's very hard to whistle when you're smiling. Only a continuous, audible whistle counts. 30 seconds is varsity duration and 45 seconds is olympic caliber.

A Lightweight Idea *

Haul out your stash of balloons. Ask each member of the group to blow up and tie off a balloon. Use a "nickel" balloon so that you can achieve an inflated size that is large enough for decent whack-it, smack-it action.

As the balloon-festooned group hangs on your every word, point out a steeplechase route that you planned out previously. In laying out the course, think OBSTACLES: trees, fences, indoor/outdoor, bleachers, ups and downs.

On a signal, have the players move to the first obstacle from a starting line and continue through the course without ever gripping their balloon. The balloon must remain airborne at all times. If the balloon touches the ground, the player either loses 15 seconds, or must repeat the previous obstacle (their choice). If a balloon breaks, the player must reach into their pocket for the single spare held in reserve. Blow-up procedure follows and the steeplechase continues.

If the second balloon breaks, that player is disqualified for the time being. "Time being," according to the bureau of weights and measures is 150 seconds (151 seconds during a leap year).

175

Compass Walk ***

Think you can walk in a straight line for the length of a football field with your eyes closed? How about 50 yards?

As it turns out, Homo sapiens do not have the migratory instincts of other mammals and you are only fooling yourself if you think your "Daniel Boone" instincts are more accurate than a compass. The following exercise is an eye-opener for most people and, in addition, serves as a useful trust-building situation. Participants are amazed at their own performances and the circuitous ramblings of their friends.

Take the group to a football-size-field (or larger) and ask a student to take a visual fix on some prominent distant object, announce the intended object, close his/her eyes and begin walking directly toward that object. Ask someone else to follow the walker to prevent injury (holes, rocks, fences) and to call an eventual halt if the walker's jaunt continues beyond the announced destination or an immovable object blocks the way. Talking between walker and guide is OK, but make sure the guide follows behind the walker so that the "way" is not inadvertently revealed.

Ask a volunteer to try this activity so that all can observe the results, then have the students pair up to try the walk themselves. There will be lots of pairs walking around, so be sure to indicate that following another blindfolded person (sound) is no assurance of reaching a destination.

The results of this purposeful meandering leads to much good-humored kidding, a feeling of trust and an opportunity for a group to further develop an activity. Participants usually enjoy experimenting with why their parabolic paths are so contrary to instinct. These are a few examples of experiments that have been tried in the past with a consistent lack of accuracy.

a. Ask two students (eyes closed) to walk arm-in-arm, or holding hands, to see if compensation or dominance plays a significant role. It is a classic sight to see two husky fellows walking arm-in-arm off into the sunset.

b. Try jogging toward a visual goal (blindfolded or with eyes closed).
c. Walk backward.
d. Ride on someone's shoulders. Both participants close their eyes. The rider gives directions; the carrier is strictly transportation in this case.
e. Try crawling. Dogs do a pretty good job of navigating accurately over long distances, and it can't be all in the nose.
f. Bring the entire group together at the end of the exercise and suggest that they try to walk as a group (physical contact) toward a goal. This blob method usually increases the accuracy, but can also initiate discord that literally ends up in two or three sub groups going their own way.

If the group stays together and ends up somewhere near their goal, ask them to stop, keep their eyes closed and then individually point to where they think the goal object is located. The crossed arms and fingers in each other's faces lends credence to the old adage, "You can't get there from here."

Human Camera *

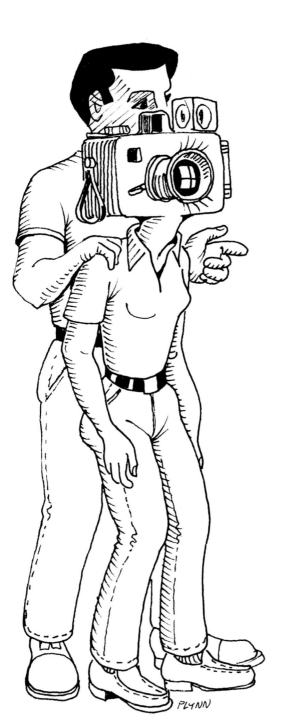

Here's a useful trick for environmental teachers or interested educators.

The teaching theme is to demonstrate how you can use a partner as a camera. After having made appropriate comments about how a camera is like a human eye, ask your partner to close his/her eyes, and then lead the partner to a spot where there is an interesting object that you would like to record on retinal film. Using the human camera body as an infinitely mobile tripod, set up your partner's head (the camera) in such a way that his/her closed eyes are directly in front of the chosen subject. Gently pull the ear lobe to activate the shutter. At this encouragement, the "camera" opens and closes the eye lids (shutter) *very* quickly in order to record the scene. Lead your partner to a few more photographic possibilities and then talk about what you two have jointly recorded.

Vary the scenes from close-ups to distant landscapes. Switch roles after you have talked about the experience with your partner or as a group. I think you can easily recognize that this is not only a shared experience of high quality, but also a trust sequence that leads to good feelings and a useful pairs' rapport.

177

178

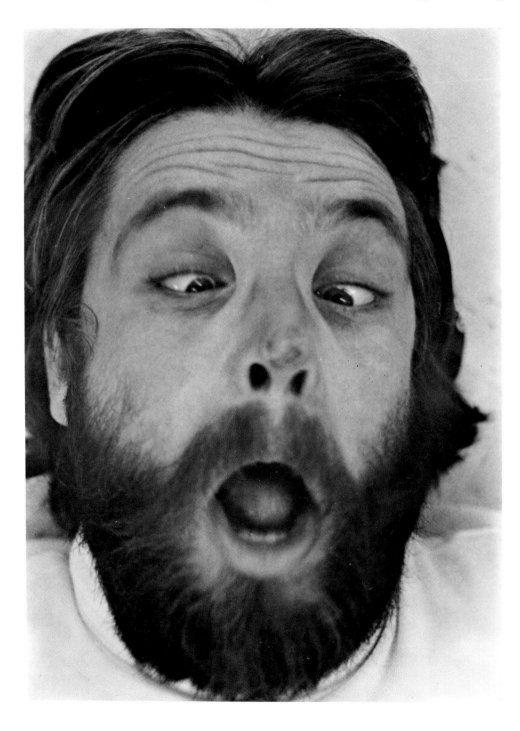

Do you ever end up with a few minutes at the end of a class with nothing for the students to do? Insert Sylvia's Silly Sequence.

To begin, lie down on your back and try to totally relax. You will find it's easier to relax lying on a wrestling mat than on a gravel road. Have someone place a penny directly on top of your nose so that it balances there in a horizontal position. Try to dislodge the coin using only facial contortions; no movement of the head or body is allowed at all. Blowing the coin off your nose displays such unbecoming gaucherie that I don't think any further comment is necessary; however, use of the tongue is an indication of rare talent indeed.

Set your own time limits, considering that two minutes of unsuccessful facial contortions seems interminable to a contestant. If you have two players that have experienced "the thrill of victory" and are looking for some head-to-head competition, ask them to lie down so that the tops of their heads are touching and begin the penny sequence from this position. Cries of "Get Crazy" and "Topple the Copper" by knowledgeable spectators add to the panoply and festive air surrounding these intense contests.

Count Off **

This activity is so simple that you may initially ignore its possibilities. Try it with a group during some down time, or if there are a few minutes before the class bell.

Ask a group of ten people (the numbers may vary, but try to have one person per number) to count to ten without pre-planning who is going to say which number, and try to do this without having two (or more) people saying the same number simultaneously. It seems easy—it isn't.

For example, anyone can begin by saying, "one," then someone else tries to sneak in a "two" and then a quick "three," "four," and then "fi...," and back to zero to begin again. How come? Two people tried to say five at the same time. Get it? Got it! Good.

Medley Relay *

179

This is a relay where the group participants compete against themselves or, more specifically, against a time or distance that they have previously established. In this case, total distance achieved by the group is the criterion.

Each member of the relay team must perform his/her best effort toward increasing the team's distance from a starting line. The performances are done in sequence; i.e., one after another, with each attempt carefully marked.

The events to choose from are as follows, but the sequence is up to you. I have found that finishing with the handstand walk provides an exciting finale. All of these events are measured from an initial starting line.

Medley Relay Events—(1) standing broad (long) jump; (2) standing backward jump; (3) side leap (one leg); (4) cartwheel; (5) dive and roll; (6) one-legged hop (right and left leg); (7) front forward flip from a stand; (8) handstand walk. Add whatever type of forward movement that seems to make sense, or more appropriately, that is well received by the group. This is an activity that becomes more enjoyable through repetition.

Mrs. O'Grady*

A genuine no prop deinhibitizer that's more fun than embarrassing.

With about 6-8 people (including yourself) standing in a circle, ask the person to your left or right the following sequence of questions and also indicate to him or her what the reply should be. This is a very traditional game.

You—"Did you hear what happened to Mrs. O'Grady?"

Other—"No, what happened?"

You—"She died."

Other—"How did she die?"

You—"With one cocked eye."

At this juncture, you close one eye tightly and hold it closed until the game is over. The person next to you who was answering your questions then asks the identical questions to the person next to her, and this continues around the circle until all the participants have "one cocked eye."

When the questioning role is yours again, continue to add embellishments to the way Mrs. O'Grady died. Example: "With her mouth awry" (and twist your mouth grotesquely to one side); "...breathing a sigh"; "...with her leg held high" (lifting one leg off the floor); and ". . . waving goodbye." By the time all of these movements, sounds and postures have been initiated and continued by all members of the circle (as the questioning creeps humorously and intermidably around from person to person) physical fatigue and a certain hysterical monotony allows an unselfconscious abandonment to the game. Why else would a semi-sophisticated adolescent stand on one leg, waving a hand absently with one eye closed, his mouth twisted to one side while emitting a series of metronome-like sighs?

If you have student leaders or another teacher that can initiate the questions, you can begin other O'Grady circles. Don't include more than 8 people in a circle for obvious reasons of physical fatigue and tedious repetition. If things are going too slowly the next time the questioning comes around to you, include "two things to do" in your obituary.

You do not debrief this "theater in the round"—simply enjoy it.

180

Peter Steele

Acknowledgements

Can you imagine having to research where all these activities came from originally? I can remember most of the ones that I dreamed up and could probably pinpoint a couple dozen more; the rest are part of the grab bag that's been around for years (and getting bigger all the time).

After offering that who-done-it disclaimer I can be more specific about thanking the people who have been helpful and integral to the writing of this collection of fun and games.

Glad and **Gus Rohnke** somehow knew when to lead and when to lay off. I'll be forever grateful for the creative atmosphere they turned me loose in and on to.

The Folks at Project Adventure, Inc. (past and present) have been consistently supportive of my writing attempts over the years and have made creative efforts seem fulfilling rather than frivolous.

And particular thanks to:

My wife, **Gloree,** for putting up with and encouraging an inveterate 47-year-old Peter Pan.

My children, **Matthew** and **Drew,** for providing an ongoing reminder of how great it can be to play for the simple and essential reason that it's fun.

Bonnie Hannable nee **Frye** for typing game ideas and garbled prose beyond understanding, and for providing humorous meaning to the ugly word expurgated.

Steve Butler, for sharing his whacky ideas and spontaneous creativity.

Elsa Martz, for proofreading a convoluted manuscript and for helping to make the text more readable for you: he/she.

Bob Nilson, for creative cartooning and machine-gun-like humor that captures a slice of life that reveals and entertains.

Plynn Williams of Wilkscraft Creative Printing, Inc. for his detailed illustrations, cartoons, exacting lay-out talents, and for sharing an occasional business beverage.

Dick Prouty for suggesting the title: **Silver Bullets,** and writing the preface.

Peter Steele for photography contributions that involved volunteering much of his own time and equipment.

Pat (Boots) Nichols for typing, finding, and tolerating.

John Cheffers for his insightful comments on risk and adventure programming.

> **Karl Rohnke** is the Executive Director of Project Adventure, Inc., located in Wenham, MA. A "Gentleman C" graduate of Washington and Lee Univ., Karl's occupational background includes, The Merchant Marine, oilfield roughneck, medical technologist, U.S. Army draftee, outdoor education and elementary classroom teacher, Outward Bound Chief Instructor, and 13 years with Project Adventure.
>
> Silver Bullets is his 4th book.

Hey straight shooter –
don't waste those Silver Bullets!

Share and pass on your best
Adventure Curriculum ideas by
sending them to "BAG OF TRICKS".

There are lots of playful buckeroos
out there just waiting for that
next slice of fun you're just settin' on.

Remember, Pardner, when it comes
to games and jollity, "Don't shade
your eyes...Plagiarize.

Adventure Notes from Karl Rohnke

P.O. BOX 77, HAMILTON, MASSACHUSETTS 01936

Bag of Tricks is a curriculum quarterly that I began writing over nine years ago to update the book *Cows' Tails and Cobras,* and to provide a vehicle for sharing of ideas in the field of adventure and experiential education.

The publishing format is simple: five photocopy sheets (both sides, single-spaced) of adventure information, mailed every three months; December, March, June and September. Quarterly features include: offbeat games and initiative problems that work; variations of the "golden oldies"; ropes course elements that exhibit pizzaz and can be put together without an engineering degree or access to big bucks; innovative ropes course construction techniques; safety considerations; idea-sharing; smatterings of a "calculated abandon" philosophy; and a few tongue-in-cheek zingers to keep things from getting too serious.

Cost for this atypical information service is $8.25 per year: four copies. If you are interested in a year's subscription, please send a check (*not* a purchase order) and your address on the form below.

★ ★ ★ ★ ★ ★ ★ ★ ★ ★ ★

Please send me a one year's subscription ($8.25 USA and Canada; $10.50 Overseas Airmail — US Funds only, payable to Karl Rohnke) for *Bag of Tricks* to:

Return to:

  Karl Rohnke
  Bag of Tricks
  P.O. Box 77
  Hamilton, MA 01936

Back issues Nos. 25 - present are available for $1.75 each; includes postage.

Name_____

Address_____

_____
(Zip, please)

Begin my subscription in: December_____March_____June_____September_____

PROJECT ADVENTURE PUBLICATIONS

If you would like to obtain additional copies of this book, the attached order form has been provided for that purpose. The project has also published several books and pamphlets in related areas. The publications are described below and can be ordered on the same form.

Books and Pamphlets

Cow's Tails and Cobras, A Guide to Ropes Courses, Initiative Games and Other Adventure Activities—This book is a revised and expanded version of Adventure Curriculum: *Physical Education*. Fully illustrated with pictures and diagrams, the book is both a curriculum guide to the Project Adventure Physical Education program and a manual for Ropes Course construction. The revised version, over 150 pages in length, includes a new chapter on group games, many new initiative problems and Ropes Course elements as well as a number of humorous cartoons and illustrations...by Karl Rohnke............... **$10.50**

Teaching Through Adventure, A Practical Approach suggests ways to use the out-of-doors and the world outside the classroom to broaden and enliven more traditional academic subjects. It gives a brief description of the elements of Adventure Curriculum, describes some examples, and includes a large section on how to develop similar programs in school systems. It is written for teachers, administrators and anyone concerned with educational change............... **$8.50**

Cranking Out Adventure, A Bike Leader's Guide to Trial and Error Touring, is based on seven years of experience with summer bike trips. The book includes such practical information as selection of students, bicycles, routes and campsites as well as descriptions of the finer points of "junking," and journal writing........... **$4.50**

Going Camping? is a basic guide for teachers taking students camping. This booklet touches on subjects that only a teacher taking students out for the first time can appreciate: ordering the bus, announcing the trip, getting the parents' permission, defining leadership and responsibility..... **$3.50**

High Profile—A how-to book on building, belaying and using indoor ropes course elements. Emphasis is on construction details. Includes climbing walls, rappel areas, tension traverse, trapeze jump, etrier passage, etc. Numerous photographs of construction and participation................... **$7.00**

Please send the following: (postage based on 1 copy, add $.50 each additional book)

_____ copies of *Cow's Tails & Cobras* @ $10.50 /copy ($2.00 postage) $_____

_____ copies of *Teaching Through Adventure* @ $8.50/copy   ($1.50 postage) $_____

_____ copies of *Cranking Out Adventure* @ $4.50/copy   ($1 postage) $_____

_____ copies of *Going Camping?* @ $3.50/copy   ($1 postage) $_____

_____ copies of *High Profile* @ $7.00/copy   ($1 postage) $_____

_____ copies of *Silver Bullets* @ 14.95/copy   ($2.00 postage) $_____

TO:_____   Postage/Handling $_____

_____   Plus .50 each additional book

_____   TOTAL $_____

_____ (zip) _____

Detach and return this sheet with a check or purchase order to Project Adventure, Inc., P.O. Box 100, Hamilton, MA 01936, (617) 468-7981

PROJECT ADVENTURE SERVICES

Project Adventure, Inc., is a national, non-profit corporation dedicated to helping schools, agencies and others to implement Project Adventure programs. Towards that end, the following services are available:

PROJECT ADVENTURE TRAINING WORKSHOPS - Through a network of national certified trainers, Project Adventure conducts workshops for teachers, counselors, youth workers and other professionals who work with people. These workshops are given in various sections of the country. Separate workshops are given in Challenge Ropes Course Skills, Counseling Skills for an Adventure-Based Program, Project Adventure Games and Initiatives, and Interdisciplinary Academic Curriculum.

CHALLENGE ROPES COURSE CONSTRUCTION - Project Adventure has been designing and constructing ropes courses (a series of individual and group challenge elements situated indoors in a gymnasium or outdoors in a grove of trees) for over 13 years. PA Staff can travel to your site and design/construct a course appropriate for your needs and budget.

CHALLENGE ROPES COURSE SOURCE BOOK - A catalog service of hard-to-find materials and tools used in the construction of Challenge Ropes Courses. This catalog also contains climbing rope and a variety of items useful to outdoor camping programs.

EXECUTIVE REACH - A management workshop for business and professional persons. This workshop is designed for increasing efficiency of team members in the workplace. The trust, communication and risk-taking ability learned in this executive clinic translate into a more cohesive and productive team at work.

For additional information, please check below and mail form to

Project Adventure, Inc.
Box 100
Hamilton, MA 01936
(617) 468-7981

____Project Adventure Training Workshops
____Challenge Ropes Course Construction
____Ropes Course Source Book
____Executive Reach
____Publications List
____Please add my name to your mailing list.

Name_____

Address_____

_____
                                    (Zip Code)